The Garden Art of Japan

THE HEIBONSHA SURVEY OF JAPANESE ART

For a list of the entire series see end of book

CONSULTING EDITORS

Katsuichiro Kamei, *art critic*
Seiichiro Takahashi, *Chairman, Japan Art Academy*
Ichimatsu Tanaka, *Chairman, Cultural Properties Protection Commission*

The Garden Art
of Japan

by MASAO HAYAKAWA

translated by Richard L. Gage

New York · WEATHERHILL/HEIBONSHA · Tokyo

This book was originally published in Japanese by Heibonsha under the title *Niwa* in the Nihon no Bijutsu Series.

First English Edition, 1973

Jointly published by John Weatherhill, Inc., 149 Madison Avenue, New York, New York, 10016, with editorial offices at 7-6-13 Roppongi, Minato-ku, Tokyo 106, and Heibonsha, Tokyo. Copyright © 1967, 1973, by Heibonsha; all rights reserved. Printed in Japan.

Library of Congress Catalogue in Publication Data: Hayakawa, Masao, 1925–/ The garden art of Japan. / (The Heibonsha survey of Japanese art) / Translation of Niwa. / 1. Gardens, Japanese—History. 2. Gardens—Japan. I. Title. II. Series. / SB458.H3813 / 712'.0952 / 72–92257 / ISBN 0–8348–1014–x

Contents

The Garden Art of Japan

CHAPTER ONE

————— • —————

The Essence of
the Japanese Garden

THE MEETING OF MAN AND NATURE It is only a small plot of ground spread with fine white gravel and planted here and there with clumps of bush clover, but the *hagi tsubo*, or bush-clover courtyard garden, at the Seiryo-den ceremonial hall of the Kyoto Imperial Palace (Figs. 1, 32) embodies the most essential elements of the whole wide and complicated world of the Japanese garden. No one who visits this place can fail to be moved by it, and no one ever tires of looking at it. Few gardens are simpler in composition, yet few inspire so deep an awareness of what is truly Japanese in the art of garden design. The bush-clover garden faces the west veranda of the Seiryo-den, while the remaining sides are enclosed by white walls. It is long in the north-south axis and completely flat. Its tranquility and elegance express quite beautifully the aesthetics and emotions of the aristocracy of the Heian period (794–1185), from which its name, if not its present physical form, dates. But what are the aspects of this small and simple garden that awaken in the viewer a profound impression of the mood of courtly times gone by and, more importantly, a deeply Japanese feeling?

The garden shows no sign of what might be called deliberate landscaping. There is no varied topography, no water, no stones, no moss. All that graces the small space is a uniform covering of white gravel and a few plants. The bush clover puts out fresh green leaf buds in early spring. After it has bloomed in autumn, it is cut back to the ground to await the coming of another springtime. We find it difficult to conceive of anything more simple.

One secret of the garden's mood is to be found in the bush clover itself. An ordinary plant seen in most fields, it by no means stands out among the flora of the country, yet for this very reason it inspires emotions that are peculiarly Japanese. Other plants, of course, produce similar effects, but in this garden of the Seiryo-den the restriction of the planting to one variety intensifies the abstract emotional appeal.

Another important factor in the appeal of the garden is the nature of the architectural setting, including the veranda of the building, its exquisitely proportioned walls, posts, and windows, and the grace of the roof with its covering of cypress-bark shingles. The mood of these elements is certainly Japanese, but the building was not constructed for the sake of the garden. In fact, the beauty of the garden derives primarily from the artlessness with which no attempt is made to elaborate on the combination of garden and building. In other words, the classic example of the

1. Bush-clover courtyard garden, Seiryo-den, Kyoto Imperial Palace.

Japanese ideal of garden form is a space in which the art itself is so artless as to be totally unapparent. Japanese gardens are places where the human heart can come into direct, pure contact with the world of plants and flowers. One of their fundamental intentions is to inspire the emotion of rejoicing with these creations of nature and of figuratively blooming when they bloom.

THE GARDEN AS
PART OF NATURE
In diametric opposition to the modesty and simplicity of the bush-clover garden at the Kyoto Imperial Palace is the Upper Garden of the Shugaku-in villa, or Shugaku-in Detached Palace, as it is officially called (Figs. 2, 6, 7, 36, 67, 68, 136). Designed by the emperor Gomizuno-o (1596–1680) and built on a site in Kyoto near the foothills of Mount Hiei, the garden achieves an

almost universal vastness of scope and a subtle combination of natural scenery and artificial landscaping that together make it one of the masterpieces of Japanese garden design. The layout takes full advantage of the hills and mountains to the north and east and the expansive open views to the south and west. A dike about 200 meters in length creates a large pond by retaining the water of two mountain streams and a branch of the Otowa River that has been directed into it. This pond (it is known as the Pond of the Bathing Dragon) and the several islands in it are the central feature of the Upper Garden. Mixed plantings on the hillside slopes and on the outer face of the dike, undulating surfaces of clipped shrubbery, waterfalls, and the islands in the pond manifest garden techniques of the highest order. But the true aim of the plan is to show to best advantage the breath-

2. *View of Upper Garden from Rin'un-tei pavilion, Shugaku-in villa, Kyoto.*

taking panorama to the west and the south: a view of the entire Kyoto Plain and of range upon range of hills and mountains stretching away into the distance.

A famous Japanese technique of garden design called *shakkei* (borrowed scenery) involves the incorporation of distant landscapes into the garden setting. The Upper Garden of Shugaku-in is often counted among the most outstanding displays of this technique. Yet its appeal is too great to be expressed in these somewhat cramped terms, for at Shugaku-in nature and garden have been so effectively united that it is difficult to tell where the work of man stops and that of nature begins. Revealing the world of nature to best effect in its purest and most beautiful forms, yet within certain spatial limits, is a basic ideal of Japanese garden design.

A SMALL MAN-MADE WORLD

Just as it did in the case of most other Japanese arts, the culture of China exerted a great influence on Japanese garden design. Buddhism, representing one of the most profound and enduring of Asian continental influences, is traditionally said to have been introduced into Japan in A.D. 552. The transformation in garden designs and techniques brought about by this momentous event is a subject of major importance. It was in the Asuka period (552–646) that Japanese garden design first turned to the concept of creating a garden as a miniature representation of the Buddhist cosmos. Such re-creations of the Buddhist universe consisted of raising a hillock to represent Mount Sumeru, the center of that universe; of making a pond to symbolize the lake Anavatapta (in Japanese, Munetsunochi); and of using rocks

3. Detail of south garden, abbot's quarters, Daitoku-ji, Kyoto.

4. *East garden of abbot's quarters, Daitoku-ji, Kyoto.*

5. Sanzon *(Buddhist triad) stone group, south garden of abbot's quarters, Daitoku-ji, Kyoto.*

in the pond to form a representation of the nine islands and eight seas of the Buddhist creation myth. In the succeeding Nara period (646–794) the basically Taoist belief in the Isles of the Blest entered Japan to take its place beside Indian-inspired Buddhist thought in the designing of gardens. According to Taoist tradition, these islands, including most notably P'eng-lai (in Japanese, Horai), were the blissful dwelling places of immortal, ageless beings. It is not surprising that people would desire to suggest an association with such happiness by placing stones in garden ponds to symbolize these felicitous places. "Islands" like these, which achieved most refined expression as

6. *View of Upper Garden, with Rin'un-tei pavilion in background and Pond of the Bathing Dragon in foreground, Shugaku-in villa, Kyoto.*

7. *View of west shore and dike, Pond of the Bathing Dragon, Upper Garden, Shugaku-in villa, Kyoto.*

stone groupings, appear in such works as the famous medieval gardening classic called the *Sakuteiki* (Treatise on Garden Making) as a basic feature of Japanese garden design. Later, with the addition of Zen thought, stone groupings came to play an even more active role in garden design, ultimately developing into the philosophically sophisticated and distinctively Japanese *kare-sansui*, or dry-landscape, garden, which typically consists of stones, gravel, a few plants, and evocations of water, although no water is employed. The south garden of the abbot's quarters at the Daitoku-ji temple in Kyoto is a classic example of the pinnacles that the *kare-sansui* style can attain (Figs. 3, 5, 33).

In one corner of the flat, rectangular, gravel-spread garden at the Daitoku-ji are arranged a number of large and small stones and some closely pruned camellia bushes in a man-made world representing the universe of Zen. The triple stone arrangement at the left end of the garden is in the *sanzon* (Buddhist triad) style and suggests a waterfall in a forest glen (Fig. 5). The carefully raked white gravel evokes images of a vast expanse of water. This attempt to create a world of contemplative thought by means of such simple natural materials as gravel, stones, moss, and other plants quite obviously stands in sharp contrast with the basic concept of the Shugaku-in garden, where the huge world of nature is incorporated virtually without alteration. Nevertheless, the simplicity of the bush-clover garden at the Kyoto Imperial Palace, the grandeur of the Shugaku-in garden, and the philosophic idealism of the stone garden at the Daitoku-ji are all rooted in the Japanese consciousness of the beauty of nature and the desire to reproduce it in gardens that embody its true essence.

CHAPTER TWO

Gardens of Early Times

ANCIENT GARDENS When was it that the Japanese first began to construct gardens? The earliest literary reference to a garden in the commonly understood sense of the word appears in the eighth-century *Nihon Shoki* (Chronicles of Japan), the second oldest of Japan's histories. Here we learn that the emperor Keiko, who came to the throne during the first century of the Christian Era, took great pleasure in the garden of his palace Kuguri no Miya and stocked its pond with carp. We also learn that during the Tumulus period (250–552) the consort of the emperor Ingyo enjoyed being alone in her palace garden. Of course we have no way of knowing what these gardens looked like. Still, since architecture and civil engineering had already developed to a certain extent and since culture from the Asian continent was filtering into Japan by way of the Korean peninsula, it is likely that the gardens were forerunners of the gardens of the Heian-period aristocracy—that is, the gardens of residences in the *shinden* style of architecture: a main building flanked by corridor-connected wings and featuring a front garden with a pond.

The Tumulus (Kofun) period takes its name from a number of keyhole-shaped grave mounds built during the approximately three centuries between 250 and 552: structures with a rectangular front and a circular rear surrounded by one or more moats. Some of these mounds are enormous, and all of them employ in their spatial composition and planning certain approaches and ideas that would have been inconceivable without a knowledge of garden design. The fact that such mounds existed when the consort of the emperor Ingyo amused herself in a garden strengthens my assumption that garden making had already achieved the status of an art by the fifth century.

During these early times, hillocks and large stones symbolizing Mount Sumeru, center of the Buddhist cosmos, appear to have been widely used. In an account of the empress Suiko, an entry for 612, the twentieth year of her reign, states that the south garden of her palace contained a bridge and a representation of this mountain. We also learn that the empress Saimei, who reigned from 655 to 661, had a garden with similar ornaments. Today, in the grounds of the Tokyo National Museum, we can see a two-piece stone carving known as the Asuka Sumeru Stone and presumably dating from the seventh century (Fig. 16). It was excavated in 1903 in the Asuka district of Nara Prefecture—the district from which the Asuka period takes its name.

The *Nihon Shoki* also tells of the garden of the famous sixth-century government minister Soga no Umako,* noting that there was an island in the garden pond and that for this reason Umako was

* The names of all premodern Japanese in this book are given, as in this case, in Japanese style (surname first); those of all modern (post-1868) Japanese are given in Western style (surname last).

8. *Detail of Tsuki no Katsura dry-landscape garden, Bofu, Yamaguchi Prefecture.*

9. *Detail of Seiryo-den and front garden, Kyoto Imperial Palace.*

10. *Detail of Shishin-den, Kyoto Imperial Palace.*

11 *(overleaf). Dry-landscape stone arrangement in upper garden, Saiho-ji, Kyoto.* ▷

12. Garden pond and stone bridge, Tenryu-ji, Kyoto.

13. *Garden pond and stone arrangements, Tenryu-ji, Kyoto.*

14. *Vacated shrine site, Ise Inner Shrine, Ise, Mie Prefecture.*

15. Iwakura *(sacred rock)* with Shinto decorations, Omiwa Shrine, Nara Prefecture.

often referred to as the Lord of the Island—an indication that the garden must have been an impressive one. It is possible to estimate the probable size and grandeur of Umako's garden from an examination of a famous grave mound where he is thought to have been interred. This mound, located in the Asuka district, is called the Stone-Stage Grave Mound because all the earth has washed away from it, leaving the stone structure of the entrance passage and the burial chamber exposed in the manner of an elevated outdoor stage (Fig. 17). The scale of the structure is surprisingly large, and the undertaking obviously required a great expenditure of money and labor. If Umako's famous garden was anywhere near as impressive, it must have been splendid indeed.

Umako's grandson Iruka was killed in the power struggle that preceded the political reforms of the Taika era (645–50), and his palace became a property of the imperial family. Known as the Palace of the Islands, it was a favorite residence of two notable imperial princes, Oama and Kusakabe, and it is mentioned in the celebrated eighth-century anthology *Man'yoshu,* particularly in the poems of Kakinomoto Hitomaro and Toneri, who speak of its garden and note that it had a bridge and a pond with a rough shoreline. We can imagine that this garden was similar in plan to the garden of the Heian-period *shinden*-style residence and to that of the Sento Imperial Palace, constructed during the Edo period (1603–1868).

Evidence like this makes it clear that the pond,

16. *Asuka Sumeru Stone, seventh century, Tokyo National Museum.*

which was to become a central feature in the composition of the traditional Japanese garden, had already been given a prominent role in the gardens of the imperial family and the aristocracy by the Asuka period. It was, however, to be greatly refined in the coming centuries.

During the Nara period, as cultural intercourse with T'ang-dynasty China increased, Japanese court architecture began to copy that of Chinese palaces, and we can surmise that garden design also imitated the T'ang style, although it is impossible to know what these Chinese-style gardens were like. Still, architecture offers some hints about the general trend of Japanese garden design during this age. While deliberately borrowing building techniques and styles, the Japanese quickly adapted them to their own land and spirit to create the distinctive *shinden* residential style. In all likelihood, gardens were purely Chinese for only a brief time before they were transformed into something closer to the Japanese heart. The garden of the Shishinden, one of the great ceremonial halls of the Kyoto Imperial Palace, suggests what an early Japanese version of a Chinese garden may have been like (Figs. 10, 22).

The eighth-century anthology *Kaifuso* contains poems that hint at the nature of Chinese influence in the Nara period, but other poems in the same collection speak of such trees as the cherry and the pine, both dearly loved by the Japanese and both widely used in Japanese gardens. Here we have an indication that Chinese tradition, even at this early time, was undergoing a process of assimilation into the Japanese culture pattern.

17. *Stone-Stage Grave Mound, seventh century, Asuka district, Nara Prefecture.*

GARDENS OF THE GODS

Certain gardenlike spaces, by being fundamentally spiritual in concept, differ in purpose from the ones that are intended to be used as places for amusement or intimacy with nature. One example of the concept of hallowed ground can be seen in the previously noted grave mounds. Of more particular interest to us here, however, are the spaces set apart as sacred to the deities of the indigenous Shinto religion.

The first appearance of the word *niwa* (garden) in Japanese literature is found in the *Nihon Shoki*, where it is used to indicate a place purified for the worship of the gods: a concept totally different from that of the garden as we think of it today. Such places no doubt resembled the *takamiya* that is still a part of the Munakata Shrine in Fukuoka Prefecture (Fig. 18): a sanctified gravel-spread area planted with a *sakaki* tree (*Cleyera ochnacea*, the sacred tree of Shinto) and reserved for the dedication of offerings to the gods.

According to Shinto belief, divinity manifests itself in all kinds of natural objects—for example, in mountains, hills, stones, and trees. We can therefore surmise that the central feature of such a sanctified area was a large stone called either the *iwakura* or the *iwasaka*—no doubt one like the giant *iwakura* that forms the center of a rock arrangement at the Omiwa Shrine on Mount Miwa in Nara Prefecture (Fig. 15). At this shrine, for which Mount Miwa itself serves as the chief object of worship, the *iwakura*, obviously preserved with the greatest of respect since ancient times, is decked with ritual straw ropes and talismans of folded

18. Takamiya *(sacred precinct)*, Munakata Shrine, Fukuoka Prefecture.

19. *Landscape engraved on a silver jar, seventh century, Shoso-in, Nara.* ▷

white paper, and the rock arrangement in which it stands reminds us of those that developed in Japanese gardens of a later age. Perhaps in the sanctified places of early days the area around such a large stone or an arrangement of stones was swept clean.

To obtain a clearer picture of the ancient sacred garden, it is worthwhile to look at the vacant site next to the one presently occupied by the Ise Inner Shrine. The two sites are used alternately for the rebuilding of the shrine at intervals of twenty years, and the plan of the compound, like those of the buildings themselves, remains substantially the same as it was in the seventh century, when the shrine is thought to have assumed its present form. Although the periodic reconstruction is carried out according to specific time-honored instructions, some alterations have inevitably crept in, but the general style has undergone no change for well over a thousand years.

Each time the shrine buildings are reconstructed, they occupy a site adjacent to the one on which the old buildings stand (Fig. 20). When the new ones are completed, a transferral ceremony is held, and the old ones are then demolished. The plot of land on which they stood is carefully cleaned and, with one exception presently to be noted, left vacant until the time for the next reconstruction arrives. It is this vacant shrine site that suggests the nature of ancient sanctified precincts.

Although I have just said that the old buildings are demolished when the new construction is completed, in fact one small post of the main shrine building is left in place and covered with a small protective shelter (Fig. 14). This post is the *shin no mihashira*—the heart post, to translate the term literally. Standing in a clean spread of white stones in a pristine forest near the sparkling waters of the Isuzu River, this small shelter contributes to a mood of sanctity that is difficult to describe but

completely unforgettable (Fig. 21). In one of his poems the twelfth-century poet-priest Saigyo speaks of being inexplicably moved to tears of gratitude at the sight, and this perhaps best expresses the feeling it evokes—a feeling that every visitor to Ise no doubt experiences. This sense of the holiness of natural beauty has figured importantly in the development of the Japanese garden.

Once the area of white stones has been occupied by the new shrine buildings and surrounded by an outer wooden wall and three inner wooden fences, a space completely different from the ancient sanctified open space is born. In a word, a garden has appeared. The emphasis is still on divinity, but it has shifted from the sacred unenclosed area to an area defined by architecture. When the elegantly simple main building, with its round posts and walls of Japanese cypress, its thick thatched roof, its elevated floor, its high railings, its crossed rafters, and its carefully placed row of ridge orna-

ments, is finished, and when the smaller accompanying buildings and finally the enclosing fences and wall stand in their appointed places, the flat area of white stones ceases to exist for itself and begins to participate in the space of the shrine. This shift from self-assertion to participation in another space marks the advent of the garden.

GARDENS OF EMPERORS From the year 794, when Kyoto became the capital, until 1868, when Tokyo superseded it in this role, the Kyoto Imperial Palace was the official residence of the emperors of Japan, but it was not the same imperial palace that we see in Kyoto today. During that long period the palace was frequently destroyed by fire, and its location often changed. The style of the buildings varied with the times in which new palaces were built and with the rarely stable financial situation of the imperial family, which was particularly impoverished in

20. *Aerial view of Ise Inner Shrine and adjacent shrine site, Ise, Mie Prefecture.*

21. *Aerial view of Ise Inner Shrine in its forest setting, Ise, Mie Prefecture.*

eras when its authority was no more than nominal or ceremonial. In the eighteenth century an earnest effort was made to employ ancient records of palace buildings in a reconstruction that would capture the appearance and mood of the Heian-period palace, but this too was destroyed by fire shortly after it was completed. The buildings as they stand at present are nineteenth-century reconstructions of the eighteenth-century palace buildings. Still, even though nothing there can be called a true relic of the remote past, the palace does suggest how the buildings and gardens of the Heian period looked.

On its south side the Shishin-den, the main official and ceremonial hall, faces an extensive courtyard spread with white gravel (Fig. 22). A staircase of eighteen steps connects the brilliant spaces of the courtyard with the dimmer ones of the veranda and the interior of the hall. On the left side of the staircase, as one faces the building, stands a mandarin-orange tree (Fig. 25); on the right, a cherry tree (Fig. 10). The courtyard, which can be entered by one of three gates—the Jomeimon on the south side, the Nikkamon on the east, and the Gekkamon on the west—is surrounded by a corridor covered with a tile roof supported on vermilion-painted columns. A stone-lined rain trough under the eaves of the corridor is filled with perpetually running clear water (Fig. 23).

West of the north garden of the Shishin-den stands the Seiryo-den, the former residence of the emperor. To the north of the Seiryo-den there once stood another building, the Jiju-den, and the compound was enclosed by a white-walled corridor, so that several courtyard gardens were created. The front garden of the Seiryo-den, like that

of the Shishin-den, is spread with white gravel and has a rain trough that runs beneath the eaves of the corridor, but here, instead of trees, there are two clumps of bamboo, each enclosed by a framework of latticed wood (Figs. 9, 24).

As we can surmise from early screen and scroll paintings (Fig. 26), the residential gardens of the Heian-period aristocrats were rather more gay and colorful than the austere gardens we have just observed. The homes of the wealthy and powerful in that age were built in the previously noted *shinden* style. The buildings faced the south and fronted on a garden with a large pond surrounded by trees and other plants and ornamented with rock arrangements and a bridge leading to an island. Guests were rowed about the pond in boats whose prows were carved to represent dragons' heads and the heads of mythical birds.

The gravel-spread gardens of the Shishin-den and the Seiryo-den clearly belong to another tradition. While the typical *shinden* garden style may be traced to the above-mentioned Palace of the Islands, the flat white-gravel garden, even though it may be stretching a point to say so, probably originated in the concept of a sacred area like that of the Ise Shrine.

In terms of architectural style as well, the Shishin-den, with its elevated floor—a characteristic ancient Japanese device—belongs in the same general current as the buildings at Ise, which are in the *shimmei,* or shrine, style. Nor is this surprising, for the emperor, regarded in the past as the human incarnation of a god, sat in the Shishin-den to conduct important ceremonies of state. Consequently, the garden too became essentially a ceremonial area. From the time of the Daigyoku-den, the great palace built in Nara when that city was the capital, Chinese styles were often copied,

◁ *22. Shishin-den and front courtyard, Kyoto Imperial Palace.*

23. Rain trough adjoining colonnade corridor, Kyoto Imperial Palace.

but the ceremonies held in the buildings were purely Japanese, and the garden spaces of these palaces naturally grew to resemble the sanctified spaces at indigenous Shinto shrines. In this development we find one of the origins of Japanese gardens or, more accurately, of Japanese garden spaces. No doubt because an imperial palace differed from a shrine, the formal style of the palace layout was Chinese, as it is at the Kyoto Imperial Palace. For instance, the roofed corridor surrounding the courtyard is certainly a continental element of the architecture. But the unfinished wood of the Shishin-den, the cypress-bark-shingle roof, the elevated floor, and, most of all, the white gravel of the courtyard—these are unmistakably Japanese, and their lineage is linked with that of the Ise Shrine.

The features of the Shishin-den and the Seiryo-den gardens that mark them as being palace rather than shrine gardens in atmosphere are the mandarin-orange tree and the cherry tree in the one and the clumps of bamboo in the other. These features bring to mind two much older and long since vanished palaces: that of the emperor Yomei (reigned 585–87) and that of the empress Saimei (reigned 655–61). Extant descriptions of these two imperial residences tell us that the wooden staircases at the front were each flanked by two zelkova trees that stood in the garden. It is impossible to know today whether these trees had mystical significance or whether they merely enhanced the beauty of the setting. Again, there is no way of discovering whether they were old trees that had long been on the site or whether the builders of the palace in each case brought them to the garden on purpose. It is certain, however, that two trees standing at the front of such buildings symbolized the nature of a palace. Since these buildings were constructed

in the sixth and the seventh centuries, they may have retained elements of the sacred shrine atmosphere and may therefore have been ornamented with the sacred straw ropes called *shimenawa*.

On the other hand, the cherry, the mandarin orange, and the bamboo in the Kyoto Imperial Palace garden as it exists today have completely lost all religious associations. Ornamental in character, they produce a feeling of gentleness more suitable to the home of a human being than to the abode of a god. It is important to note, however, that this feeling of gentleness is tinged with a certain austerity that sets it apart from the sweet and carefree emotion evoked by the bush-clover garden of the same palace. Again, the lattice fences surrounding the plants in the gardens of the Shishinden and the Seiryo-den play an important role in preserving the unemotional dignity of the garden spaces. This is especially true of the fences around

the two plantings of bamboo (Fig. 24), for great skill has been employed to harmonize the proportions of the latticework with the scale of the plants and the placidity and massiveness of the architecture. As a result, these simple fences highlight the entire space. In fact, the very care with which the designer planned fences that do nothing more than surround clumps of bamboo suggests that perhaps a certain mystical significance still attaches to these plants in spite of their having a predominantly decorative function.

POND GARDENS OF THE HEIAN AGE Today, unfortunately, not a single true *shinden* garden survives to show how splendid the style once was, but from extant records and picture scrolls and screens (Fig. 26) it is possible to arrive at an idea of how such gardens looked. In contrast with the sedate cere-

◁ *24. Detail of front courtyard showing fence-enclosed ornamental bamboos, Seiryo-den, Kyoto Imperial Palace.*

25. Detail of front courtyard garden showing mandarin-orange tree, Shishin-den, Kyoto Imperial Palace.

monial gardens of the Kyoto Imperial Palace, the residential gardens of the Heian aristocrats were brighter and more relaxed-looking places that invariably featured a large pond. These gardens ran to considerable size, as one can tell from a description of the Shinsen-en, which was built at the end of the eighth century and is considered to have been one of the most representative gardens in the *shinden* style.

Kyoto was originally laid out in orderly blocks of the kind that characterized the great capital cities of China. Each of these blocks, called a *cho*, was about 120 meters to a side. Residential plots were measured in *cho*, and the amount of land allotted to a given person depended on his official rank and his social status. The Shinsen-en garden extended to a total of eight of these *cho* units: two on the east-west side and four on the north-south side. In all likelihood a garden of this size made

maximum use of the natural topography and vegetation, at the same time featuring a pond and a central island, both of which may have been artificially created. The meager northeast corner of the Shinsen-en pond that remains today gives a small hint of the former magnificence of the garden.

The early *shinden*-style mansions of the aristocrats closely copied their Chinese models. The main building faced south, and the subsidiary buildings were arranged symmetrically on its right and left sides. Gradually, however, the Japanese personality manifested itself in asymmetrical placements and in such subtle alterations as a shift from heavy-hinged reticulated wooden shutters (*shitomido*) to light paper-filled panels (*shoji*), the use of grass mats to cover the entire floors of rooms instead of serving as occasional cushions for sitting, and the installation of ceilings to conceal the formerly exposed interior roof structures. All these changes

26. *Detail from screen painting show-ing* shinden-*style garden,* Jingo-ji, *Kyoto.*

constituted a transition from the ancient *shinden* to the later *shoin* residential style, but one must remember that the complete shift required four centuries. That is to say, the *shinden* style, as adapted by the Japanese, so well suited their tastes and needs that they were quite long in giving it up entirely. Moreover, the *shinden*-style use of ponds and islands in gardens that harmonized with adjacent buildings attained so high a level of perfection that no major revolution in the general layout ever took place.

The gardens of early-Heian aristocrats represented a eulogy of the imperial court and the political system of which it formed the center. Later the Pure Land, or Jodo, sect of Buddhism and its concept of a paradise to which the faithful would go after death gradually attained influence over the aristocrats and came to be reflected in

their architectural and landscape designs. The reason for the popularity of the religion is not far to seek. As the Heian social structure grew older, it revealed serious flaws that ultimately spelled its downfall. But a period of great disturbances intervened before a new government dealt the old system its deathblow. During the intermediary age of troubles, disappointed and discouraged aristocrats turned to Pure Land Buddhism because it offered the hope of salvation and entrance into the Western Paradise of Amida Buddha after death. Their residential gardens, like those of their temples, often represented attempts to re-create on earth the ethereal splendors of Amida's paradise. In other words, the garden became a place of consolation and hope for people subjected to uncertainty and danger in their daily lives.

The central feature of such building-and-garden

27. *Pond and stone groups at site of Motsu-ji, Hiraizumi, Iwate Prefecture.*

complexes was an Amida Hall, a structure that housed an image of Amida Buddha. Today, by good fortune, we still have several buildings and their gardens that have survived from the Heian age to give us an idea of what these representations of Amida's paradise were like. Among them are the Joruri-ji, with its nine images of Amida, and the exquisite Phoenix Hall of the Byodo-in.

The celebrated aristocrat Fujiwara Yorimichi (992–1074) built the Phoenix Hall, as it is called today, to serve as the Amida Hall of his villa at Uji, not far from Kyoto. Although the garden is now a far cry from what it was many centuries ago, the building makes it easy to imagine the grace of the original setting. The structure itself, which faces a pond (Fig. 28), is supposed to resemble a phoenix about to take flight. The main section represents the bird's body; the two connecting side

pavilions, the wings; and the rearward extension, the tail. The roof is surmounted by two phoenixes of gilded bronze, and the whole structure is attractively reflected in the pond. The lightness and elegance of the exterior and the rich though now sadly faded décor of the interior, together with the remnant of the pond, evoke a vision of an ancient garden where rainbow-hued lotus blossoms floated on a pond around whose shores countless small birds sang their tranquil songs. When the golden light touches the vermilion columns and the large gilded statue of Amida, one feels that here indeed is a corner of the Western Paradise.

The Joruri-ji, perhaps because of its location deep in the mountains near the boundary between Kyoto and Nara prefectures, is as subdued and dark-looking as the Phoenix Hall is airy and bright. The main hall of the temple, which houses nine

28. *Phoenix Hall and garden pond, Byodo-in, Uji.*

statues of Amida, is said to have been built in the mid-twelfth century by the priest Eshin, son of Fujiwara Tadamichi. The nature of this undertaking and the formal design of the architecture and garden (Fig. 29) indicate a deepening both of faith in Amida and of philosophic content since the days when another Fujiwara, the regent Michinaga (966–1027), had built the temple known as the Hojo-ji. Although the Joruri-ji pond is now sadly ravaged, it is still filled with water lilies that bloom year after year. The gentle dignity of the nine Amida statues has not altered with the passing of the centuries. The somber, unworldly calm of this temple is not so much the product of the working of time as a reflection of the spiritual world outlook of the priest Eshin.

In addition to the main family residing in and around Kyoto, there were many Fujiwara branch families in various parts of the country. The famous Chuson-ji, the Kanjizaio-in, and the Muryoko-in are all examples of temples with Amida Halls built in or around Hiraizumi in Iwate Prefecture by the Oshu, or northern, branch of the family in the days of its grandeur—that is, the twelfth century. Another such Fujiwara temple was the Motsu-ji, also located in Hiraizumi. It was destroyed by fire in 1226, rebuilt, and then again destroyed by fire in 1573, and today nothing remains of its pagodas, colonnades, and halls. But the pond, with its tree-lined shores and its rock arrangements (Figs. 27, 30), survives to tell us something of the garden techniques employed during the late Heian period.

It is true that in basic philosophical concept the *shinden*-style gardens and those of such Amida tem-

29. *Main hall and garden, Joruri-ji, Kyoto Prefecture.*

ples as the Byodo-in and the Joruri-ji differ vastly, but from the standpoint of garden technique they are not very far apart. In both, the aristocratic and courtly fondness for ponds that harmonize with architecture plays a major role. Moreover, the same basic techniques are used in both to treat shorelines and groupings of rocks, stones, and plants. As a matter of fact, ever since the days of Soga no Umako, Lord of the Island, ponds and islands have been a garden ideal. The predilection for them has persisted to the present, although the techniques of their construction and design have been greatly refined over the centuries. The high level of skill displayed in the stone groups in and around the pond of the Motsu-ji, so distant from Kyoto, suggests the still greater sophistication of landscaping techniques in the capital city itself.

The famous garden classic *Sakuteiki* (Treatise on Garden Making), which deals with the planning and construction of gardens for *shinden*-style mansions, reveals the extent to which the men responsible for the aristocratic residential garden understood their work. The *Sakuteiki* was written by Tachibana Toshitsuna (1027–94), a son of the same Fujiwara Yorimichi who built the Phoenix Hall. Some two centuries later—in 1289, to be exact—it was furnished with a supplement, so that it is now considered to be a work in two volumes. Toshitsuna's original book, a compilation of the considerable knowledge of garden design and construction that he had amassed over many years of observation and actual experience in garden making, touches on everything from *shinden*-style layout and composition to details of the treatment of

30. *Stone groups in former pond garden at site of Motsu-ji, Hiraizumi, Iwate Prefecture.*

ponds, streams, islands, bridges, waterfalls, and plants. The discussion of stone groups reflects a degree of aesthetic sensibility and profound experience that is truly surprising.

GARDENS OF ARISTOCRATIC VILLAS As we have noted earlier, Kyoto—and for that matter Nara before it—was planned in the regular checkerboard pattern typical of Chinese capital cities, notably Ch'angan. For this reason the construction of vast gardens like the Shinsen-en was generally impossible. In order to lay out large areas with villas or lodges where they could enjoy the world of nature, the aristocrats were forced to find sites in the suburbs of the capital. And this, indeed, they often did, for a love of the beauty of nature and a desire to escape from the bustle of town life had become

deeply ingrained characteristics of the Japanese spirit even before the time when similar sentiments were introduced along with Chinese poetry, especially the poetry of the T'ang period. It was because a spiritual affinity of this kind existed between the national characters of Japan and China that the Japanese easily absorbed and assimilated Buddhism and Confucianism as well as the art and literature of the Chinese. But in the process of borrowing, they always altered and adapted their acquisitions to produce a new and truly Japanese culture from imported elements.

In the capital city of Nara the aristocrats built splendid residences in the Chinese style and gave them such names as Mansion of Treasures and Treasure Tower, but they also built less ostentatious dwellings on the outskirts of the city. We know, for example, that the eighth-century statesman and

31. *Detail of dry-landscape garden, Ryoan-ji, Kyoto.*

32. Bush-clover courtyard garden (hagi tsubo), *Seiryo-den, Kyoto Imperial Palace.*

33. Dry-landscape garden, abbot's quarters, Daitoku-ji, Kyoto. ▷

34. *Detail of dry-landscape garden, abbot's quarters, Daisen-in, Daitoku-ji, Kyoto.*

35. *View of garden and pond from Golden Pavilion, Rokuon-ji, Kyoto.*

36 *(overleaf). Upper Garden (Kami no Chaya)* ▷
and borrowed scenery, Shugaku-in villa, Kyoto.

37. *Detail of garden attributed to Sesshu, Joei-ji,*
Yamaguchi City, Yamaguchi Prefecture.

38. *Detail of dry-landscape garden attributed to* ▷
Kano Motonobu, Taizo-in, Myoshin-ji, Kyoto.

39. Stone group in garden attributed to Murata Juko, Shinju-an, Daitoku-ji, Kyoto.

40. *Detail of dry-landscape garden, Reiun-in, Myoshin-ji, Kyoto.*

41. *Dry-landscape garden, abbot's quarters, Konchi-in, Nanzen-ji, Kyoto.*

42. *Arashiyama viewed from Katsura River, Kyoto.*

poet Prince Nagaya invited the empress Gensho and the emperor Shomu to enjoy the rural pleasures of his villa at Saho, for both of his imperial visitors have left poems in praise of this country retreat in the celebrated anthology *Man'yoshu,* where they speak of its dark wood and its thatched roof. The dark wood was no doubt natural-log posts with the bark left on, and the roof of the villa was most likely of miscanthus thatch. To eyes accustomed to the Chinese-style splendors of the capital, the simplicity, novelty, and rusticity of this country retreat must have been extremely appealing. The gardens of such rural residences probably took full advantage of the natural topography and may well have commanded sweeping views of the hills and mountains around Nara. Prince Nagaya, whose wife was the daughter of Prince Kusakabe, was himself a son of Prince Takechi, who in turn was a son of the

emperor Temmu and who distinguished himself as a soldier, statesman, and poet. Consequently, Nagaya was brought up in the highest social circles of his time. He had a deep interest in both architecture and garden design, and his predilection for these subjects was inherited by such later imperial figures as the emperor Saga (reigned 809–23) and the emperor Gomizuno-o (reigned 1611–29), both of whose names ornament the history of the Japanese garden.

Osawa Pond, in northwestern Kyoto, is a memento of the emperor Saga and his villa Saga-in, built there in the early ninth century as a rural retreat for him following his retirement from the throne. In contrast with such urban gardens as Shinsen-en, whose palatial buildings in Chinese style reached the acme of splendor, the Saga-in and its garden were obviously built to fulfill the re-

43. Osawa Pond at site of Saga-in villa, Kyoto.

quirements of the retired emperor for a setting of natural beauty and rustic tranquility like that of Prince Nagaya's villa at Saho on the outskirts of Nara. After the emperor's death in 842, the villa became the temple Daikaku-ji, dedicated to prayers for his happiness in the next world and to the preservation of the beauty of the pond.

This pond, known today as Osawa no Ike, or Osawa Pond (Fig. 43), has an area of some 20,000 square meters. It was created by building a dam about four meters high to hold back the waters of a nearby stream. At its north end rises Mount Asahara, whose elegant shape is reflected in the water. Along the side running from east to south is a distant view of the Kyoto Plain. Although it is conceived on a large scale, the pond is by no means pompous in style. It belongs to the lofty imperial tradition later embodied in the garden of the

Shugaku-in villa, designed and built by the emperor Gomizuno-o in the mid-seventeenth century.

The buildings of the Saga-in are thought to have stood on a rise northeast of the pond, but nothing remains of them today. Some garden stones, however, still stand around the so-called central island in the northern reach of the pond and around the islands called Tenjin and Kiku. In addition, a stone group thought to be the remains of the garden's Nakoso Waterfall can be seen a short distance to the north of the pond. This waterfall was still famous enough, some two hundred years later, to be the subject of a poem in the anthology *Hyakunin Isshu,* but it had already fallen into ruin at that time, as the poem itself indicates. Nevertheless, even today one may still be charmed by the beauty of the gentle mountains in the vicinity of the now vanished Saga-in and, at the same time,

44. *Approach to Kozan-ji, Kyoto.*

perhaps experience emotions like those that the setting once evoked in the hearts of the emperor and his court.

Not far from this site, on the shore of Hirosawa Pond, the tenth-century priest Kancho (Hirosawa Sojo), grandson of the emperor Uda, built the temple known as the Henjo-ji on a spot famous for its views of the moon. It was also in this same general vicinity that Prince Iyo, son of the emperor Kammu, built his villa on a site along the Oi River that commanded a view of the greatly admired scenery of Arashiyama (Fig. 42). More than four centuries later, on this same land, the emperor Gosaga built his Kameyama Palace.

Although the Sekisui-in of the Kozan-ji temple is of a later period than the gardens and villas mentioned above, it offers some hints of the way in which buildings were devised to fit harmoniously into gardens whose primary purpose was to embrace views of natural scenery and thus to permit communication with the great world of nature. The Kozan-ji is located at Togano-o, northwest of Kyoto, in the same mountainous area as Takao, which is famous for its autumn maples. The temple is best known for its ownership of one of the treasures of Japanese art: the *Scroll of Frolicking Animals* by the priest-painter Toba Sojo (1053–1140). A visitor to the Kozan-ji in autumn carries away an unforgettable impression of the beauty of the maples and the bright-colored fallen leaves strewn over the path that leads upward to the temple (Fig. 44). Along one side of this path a stone wall surmounted by a low wall of clay with a tile top winds through the grove of trees. It is an altogether excellent approach.

The Sekisui-in, the oldest building at the temple,

45. View from Sekisui-in, Kozan-ji, Kyoto.

46. *Mountain scenery of Takao, with Jingo-ji at right, Kyoto.*

was moved here in the thirteenth century from another location by the Buddhist saint Myoe. It is almost impossible to suppress a gasp of surprise at the loveliness of the view from the veranda of this building (Fig. 45). Far below in the distance flows the sparkling Kiyotaki River, and in the background stretches a range of gently rounded mountains. Beginning with Myoe and continuing through a large number of head priests and countless visitors, people have found the variety of views from the veranda an inexhaustible source of pleasure: fresh spring greenery, rich autumn foliage, a tranquil moon rising over the rim of the mountains.

The relation between architectural space and natural views at the Sekisui-in can only be called direct. There is nothing in this instance of the

shakkei, or borrowed-scenery, technique—that is, the technique by which distant mountains or other scenic elements are integrated with the garden setting or with interior spaces in a landscape composition. Without the intermediary effect of any garden-design techniques, obvious planning, ponds, or clay walls, the architectural spaces are suddenly and startlingly connected with the natural vista. The poetic spirit that composed this space must have predated the thirteenth century, when, as we have noted, the Sekisui-in was moved to its present location. In fact, the same direct relation between building and nature is to be observed in numerous mountain retreats dating from as early as the Nara period. A similar sudden juxtaposition of architectural space and vast natural scene is found at the Heian-period temple Jingo-ji (Fig. 46).

CHAPTER THREE

Buddhist Gardens
of the Medieval Age

THE NATURAL TALENTS OF MUSO SOSEKI As expressed in the gardens of the aristocrats from ancient to medieval times, the spirit of adapting to nature and of loving and respecting it throughout the changes of the seasons is not only a distinguishing trait of the Japanese but has also been a fundamentally decisive factor in the development of the Japanese garden. Obviously the topography of Japan and the beauty of its natural scenery were basic to the growth of this spirit.

The *Sakuteiki,* of which we have already taken note, clearly expresses the spirit of landscape gardening rooted in a love of natural scenery. At the beginning of its outline of garden essentials, it states that one must visit the famous scenic spots of the various provinces of Japan to absorb and master their beauty so that they can later be given soft and modified form in garden design. This is the general policy of the book, which goes on to examine with keen aesthetic discernment the actual techniques of expressing seas, mountains, waterfalls, and streams in landscaping terms. The technical explanations in the *Sakuteiki* are dominated by detailed descriptions of ways to represent mountain streams realistically, but this is as it should be, since reproducing the beauty of such streams in a garden presents more difficulties than constructing

more conspicuous elements like ponds to represent lakes or seas, rock groups to represent mountains, and waterfalls to represent natural cataracts. To make a waterfall, for example, one need only provide a source of water and a stone for it to fall over. To produce a pond requires only a suitable depression and, again, a source of water. But the techniques involved in creating a beautiful stream are more demanding. The *Sakuteiki* tells the prospective designer that the bed of a garden stream must be varied to suggest first a rivulet racing through a narrow cleft in the mountains, then a gently moving or eddying passage of water, and then a larger body of water into which the stream is finally incorporated. While the text of the book reveals perceptive observations of nature and an impressive accumulation of technical landscaping skill and experience, it goes beyond this level to suggest the spirit of an artist grappling with difficult problems of expression. Because even people not directly connected with the design and construction of gardens can understand and appreciate this spirit, the precepts of the *Sakuteiki* have long remained the standards of Japanese garden composition. That its concepts have lived in the minds of Japanese landscape designers for many centuries is clear from the beautiful stream and pond in the garden of the Murin-an in Kyoto (Fig. 143)—a

47. *Pond and* yodomari ishi, *or night mooring stones, suggesting a line of boats anchored for the night, lower garden, Saiho-ji, Kyoto.*

garden of the Meiji era (1868–1912) that vividly manifests the spirit of the *Sakuteiki*. (This garden will be described in a later chapter.)

The great Buddhist priest Muso Soseki (1275–1351), who was awarded the title Muso Kokushi, or Muso the National Teacher, is the most important figure in medieval Japanese gardening. Although he belonged to the tradition of the *Sakuteiki* and its emphasis on the representation of streams in gardens, Muso breathed fresh life into this tradition and brought a vigorous new aesthetic quality into the gardens of his time. Much of his fame as a landscape expert rests on the design of the garden of the Kyoto temple Saiho-ji, commonly known as the Moss Temple (Koke-dera) because of its luxuriant ground cover of many different kinds of moss.

In 1339, Muso was commissioned by the noble-man Fujiwara Chikahide to convert the Saiho-ji from a Jodo-sect temple to a Zen temple. Although the pronunciation of the name Saiho-ji remained unaltered, Muso changed one of the Chinese char-acters with which it was written, thereby changing the meaning from Temple of the Western Direction to Temple of the Western Fragrance. In the process of conversion, Muso completely altered the appear-ance of the temple by building halls and pavilions and redesigning the garden. Today none of his buildings remain, although some of them, having been destroyed in the course of time, were rebuilt in later ages. The garden (Figs. 11, 47, 49–51, 53, 54, 58) has also changed considerably, but the outline of the Golden Pond (Fig. 47) still suggests the general plan of the garden in its vicinity, and

48. *Musai Bridge and Garyu Pond, Eiho-ji, Toyo-oka, Gifu Prefecture.*

49. *Stone group with sacred stone (upper right) and dry* ▷
stream (foreground) in upper garden, Saiho-ji, Kyoto.

the dry-landscape garden (Figs. 11, 54) near the Shito-an teahouse for the most part preserves its original appearance. These two areas of the garden display Muso's skill in design at its best.

A gate called the Kojokan (Fig. 50) divides the Saiho-ji garden into two different worlds: the spacious garden centered on the Golden Pond and the upper dry-landscape garden. Although the present subdued serenity of the pond, the mosses, and the trees gives no hint of it, this part of the garden is said to have been both ostentatious and extremely beautiful in its original form. Its dynamic composition, a complete departure from the older *shinden*-style residential garden and the Jodo-style temple layout, included a two-story pavilion called the Ruri-den on the north shore of the pond, tea-houses like the Tampoku-tei and the Shonan-tei, a pavilioned bridge, and a boathouse for the excursion craft used on the pond. It is possible to imagine

how new and striking the Ruri-den pavilion must have been if one realizes that the Golden Pavilion at the Rokuon-ji (Fig. 55) and the Silver Pavilion at the Jisho-ji were patterned after it. The Musai Bridge over the Garyu Pond at the Eiho-ji in Gifu Prefecture (Fig. 48), also said to have been designed by Muso, gives an idea of what the bridge in the Saiho-ji garden may have been like. The teahouses of Muso's day were basically Chinese in style, but the Edo-period (1603–1868) rebuilding of the Sho-nan-tei that presently stands in the garden belongs to a later, more subdued tradition—the *wabi* school of tea—and is therefore totally unlike the teahouse Muso built.

The buildings that stood around the pond in Muso's reconstruction of the Saiho-ji garden were of the so-called Chinese style (*kara-yo*)—a style that was learned during the Kamakura period (1185–1336) by Japanese Zen monks sojourning

in Sung-period China and was often employed for Zen buildings in Japan. Clerics who made pilgrimages to China not only studied the precepts of Zen but also pursued courses of learning in many cultural fields where, true to the spirit of their day, they sought novelty and a break with the past. A work called the *Muso Kokushi Nempu* (Chronology of Muso the National Teacher) says that the halls and other buildings of the Saiho-ji were connected by twisting covered corridors that suggested the Great Wall of China—another example of the continental style of Muso's reconstruction of the Saiho-ji as a Zen temple.

It is also important to note that the paths around the pond made the Saiho-ji garden a stroll garden —that is, a garden in which one enjoys ever changing views of the landscape as he strolls through its spaces. This, like Muso's other innovations, was a new departure, since gardens of the older *shinden*

style and those of the out-of-town villas of the Heian-period aristocrats had been designed to be viewed either from the interior of a building or from excursion boats floating on a pond. It seems that this novelty was inspired largely by the newly imported Chinese fashion of drinking tea. Whereas such aristocratic pastimes of earlier days as poetry parties and musical entertainments had required one kind of landscape art for their setting, parties held for the purpose of drinking tea and savoring its pleasures made different demands on garden design. Although the tea ceremonies of Muso's time still centered on tasting and identifying different kinds of tea and had not yet developed into the refined and subtle tea ceremony of later centuries, they were part of the tradition that eventually produced the tea-garden style and the celebrated garden of the Katsura villa, the pinnacle of Japanese landscape art of its kind.

THE SPIRITUAL MEANING OF STONES

The pond garden of the Saiho-ji, although it boldly incorporated new Chinese-style elements and thereby excited both wonder and admiration in the people of that day, was based on an older garden in the Jodo-sect style and was rather deeply colored by the Heian tradition, as elements like the pond and the stream suggest. The north part of the garden, however, is something quite different. Just inside the gate called the Kojokan rises a rough stone staircase (Fig. 50) leading to a stone arrangement entirely unlike anything else in the garden (Figs. 11, 54). Here, in the upper garden, a world of chill aridity represents a crystallization of the spirit of the great priest Muso Soseki—a spirit that truly revolutionized Japanese garden design in the medieval age.

The numerous and powerful stones that dominate the central slope of the hill are placed to suggest immovable resistance against the pounding of a mighty waterfall and the frantically dashing currents at its base. Although there is not a drop of water in this dry-landscape garden of huge stones, the spatial composition seems to make the viewer's ears ring with the roar of a great flood. The stone arrangement has withstood six centuries of all kinds of weather without losing its power. What is the significance of this awe-inspiring energy? What was Muso's intention in devoting his whole heart to this kind of expression?

In earlier gardens considerable skill was expended on designing stone arrangements to accompany waterfalls and ponds, but all of these were clearly imitations of nature: reconstructions of

50 (opposite page). Kojokan gate and steps leading to upper garden, Saiho-ji, Kyoto.

51 (above). Stone group representing Mount Sumeru, Saiho-ji, Kyoto.

52. Waterfall stone arrangement, Tenryu-ji garden, Kyoto.

53. North garden of Tampoku-tei teahouse, Saiho-ji, Kyoto.

natural scenery intended to give pleasure to the viewer. The stone arrangement in the upper garden of the Saiho-ji belongs to a completely different world of abstract forms. Its symbolically represented waterfall is more violent than real ones, and its dry stream is faster than those found in nature. In no more than a group of stones Muso Kokushi expressed the passion of moving waters. But the content of the design is much greater than this: it is the passion that raged in the heart of a great man who, at the time when he created this garden, was more than sixty years old. He lived in a Japan torn by civil strife, divided between two rival imperial courts, and filled with suffering and insecurity. All of this is reflected in the power and the controlled dynamics of this small garden.

In the turbulent social conditions of the medieval age, many Japanese turned to Zen Buddhism as the sole hope of salvation and strength. Among them was the priest Muso, whose early training had been in the Tendai sect of Esoteric Buddhism. As a symbol of Muso's spiritual victory over the misery of the world, the stone garden on the hill is the antithesis of the pond garden, which stands for the glorious and joyful land of salvation envisioned by the Jodo sect. In contrast with the happiness offered by the ideal beauty of a garden filled with the pride of blossoming cherry trees, the upper garden embodies a more stern and rigorous philosophy. At the Saiho-ji, then, it is possible to observe in proximity two strongly differing views of the human condition: the deeply ascetic outlook of

54. *Stone arrangements in upper garden, Saiho-ji, Kyoto.*

55. Golden Pavilion and garden pond, Rokuon-ji, Kyoto.

Zen, which sought to conceal emotion and transmute it into internal energy through rigid discipline to produce a strong and lofty spirit, as expressed in the upper garden, and the more comforting, optimistic, and beauty-filled view represented by the pond garden.

As an expression of the inner spirit of Muso Kokushi, the garden beyond the Kojokan gate does not welcome the intrusion of outsiders. In fact, it is likely that this part of the temple garden was reserved for special religious discipline from which the laity was excluded. This may explain why numerous old works praising the Saiho-ji and its setting mention only the lower garden and its pond.

Nonetheless, the extraordinary aesthetic skill of the stone arrangement clearly reveals Muso's natural talents. We do not know where he learned the techniques for grouping large numbers of stones with sharply prominent outlines, but it is certain that the perception of forms involved here goes far beyond any of the designs explained in the *Sakutei-ki*. Indeed, the spatial composition, unlike anything ever tried before, is filled with a creative spirit so strong that it continues to reverberate even in the hearts of people who view it today.

The famous present-day architect and writer Sutemi Horiguchi has said that the unusual appeal of the upper stone garden of the Saiho-ji can be traced back to the sacred precincts and the stone-and-gravel arrangements of Shinto shrines, but I frankly wonder whether one is justified in finding a similarity between the world of the shrine and the Zen world of Muso. To be sure, in both cases a sympathy between stones and the inner world of human emotions is apparent, and in the case of the

56. *Garden and pond viewed from Golden Pavilion, Rokuon-ji, Kyoto.*

large stones found in shrine compounds something surpassing humanity can be sensed. In the Saiho-ji garden, too, Muso has used stones as an embodiment of victory over human suffering. But there is a very important difference. The emotions inspired by the stones in shrine gardens are those of reverence before something created by nature. Those awakened by Muso's garden, on the other hand, center upon respect for the results of human creativity. In both instances, physical form and the human heart produce mutual reverberations. The point of departure is a matter of precedence. In the shrine garden, the natural form precedes the emotional reaction to it. In Muso's garden, the human emotion comes first, since it is deliberately expressed in the form. This very issue is the origin of art as well as a demonstration of the greatness of Muso himself.

According to traditional Buddhist cosmology, as we have noted, Mount Sumeru is the center of the universe. It is often represented in one way or another in Buddhist art. At the Saiho-ji, on the left side of the path leading from the Kojokan gate to the Shito-an teahouse, is a stone group representing the mountain (Fig. 51). Although the form of this group is more vigorous than is usual in representations of Mount Sumeru, for this very reason it comes closer to achieving a shape suitable to a mountain that is the center of the universe. The beautiful mosses around it evoke a rich image of the seas that are said to surround the mythical mountain.

Near a spring where Muso is said to have rested after exhausting sessions of *zazen* (sitting in Zen meditation) is a stone arrangement consisting of the Zazen Seki, as it is called, and a number of

57. *Moon-facing Mound, garden of Silver Pavilion, Jisho-ji, Kyoto.*

58. *Zazen Seki and accompanying stones, upper garden, Saiho-ji, Kyoto.*

59. Ocha no I stone arrangement in garden of Silver Pavilion, Jisho-ji, Kyoto.

other stones (Fig. 58). This stone group and another one (thought to have been copied from it) around a spring at the site of the vanished Soso-tei teahouse in the garden of the Silver Pavilion—the so-called Ocha no I group (Fig. 59)—are of great historical importance, for they are prototypes of the ritual stone water basin in the tea garden.

THE GOLDEN PA-VILION AND THE SILVER PAVILION

The dazzling beauty of the Saiho-ji garden entranced contemporary aristocrats and military leaders alike. No one was more taken with this beauty than Ashikaga Yoshimitsu (1358–1408), the shogun who brought an end to the disturbances that had plagued the country during the era of the rival courts and who thus firmly established the rule of the Ashikaga shogunate. In the evening years of his life Yoshimitsu built for himself a retreat in Kyoto called the Kitayama-dono, deriving many of the basic ideas for it from the Saiho-ji. This was the villa that even today reflects the glory of Yoshimitsu in the building known as the Golden Pavilion. The estate is now the temple Rokuon-ji or, more popularly, Kinkaku-ji (Temple of the Golden Pavilion).

The land on which Yoshimitsu built his villa had been the site of a great temple built and patronized by Saionji Kintsune, a thirteenth-century leader of great power and influence with the Kamakura shogunate. In fact, Kintsune's temple was so splendid that it has been compared with a magnificent temple called the Hojo-ji, built by Fujiwara Michinaga, the eleventh-century regent noted for the

lavishness of his architectural undertakings. A little more than a century after the time of Kintsune, however, the Saionji family suffered serious reverses, and the once splendid temple fell into disrepair and dilapidation. It was roughly at this time that Ashikaga Yoshimitsu obtained the site for his own use.

Yoshimitsu's general plan for the villa was to retain the existing pond and temple halls and to center the entire layout on a three-story building patterned after the Ruri-den at the Saiho-ji. This building is the famous Golden Pavilion (Fig. 55), so called because the exterior surfaces of its two upper stories are covered with gold leaf. Yoshimitsu also planned to build an elevated bridge-corridor to connect the second-story veranda of the Golden Pavilion with that of the then existent neighboring pavilion called the Tenkyo-kaku.

In front of the Golden Pavilion is a pond known as the Kyoko, or Mirror Lake (Figs. 35, 56), in which various stone arrangements were placed to create a representation of the nine mountains and eight seas of the Buddhist creation myth. Other stone groups, together with several islands and of course the glittering Golden Pavilion itself, cast their attractive reflections on the surface of the pond. In addition to the concept of this splendid pond, the Kitayama villa borrowed another element from the plan of the Saiho-ji: a teahouse at the top of a hill—in this case the Kan'un-tei, which copies the Saiho-ji teahouse Shukuen-tei at the top of the hill where the dry-landscape garden lies.

Yoshimitsu, embellishing the *shinden*-style garden of Saionji Kintsune's temple with splendors and novelties inspired by Muso Soseki's garden at the Saiho-ji, devoted all the resources of his wealth and

60. *View of garden from guest room of abbot's quarters, Tenryu-ji, Kyoto.*

power to the creation of his magnificent Kitayama estate. The original Golden Pavilion survived until 1950, when it was destroyed by fire. It has since been rebuilt and covered with the same dazzling gold leaf that ornamented its predecessor when it was first built. Today, glittering almost too gorgeously in the light of the late afternoon sun, it vividly impresses the viewer as a symbol of Japan's medieval age and of the man who played a vital role in the history of that age.

The aesthetics of medieval Japan as expressed in the Saiho-ji and the Golden Pavilion originated in a spirit of latitude amounting almost to license—a spirit produced by the vibrant energy of people who tried to counter the insecurity, doubts, and sufferings of their war-torn times through lavishness, pride, and extravagance. Their world was entirely different from the gentle world of the "sorrow of

things" as represented in the celebrated Heian-period novel *The Tale of Genji*. But when the energy of this latitude bordering on license was turned inward, it produced a number of departures in art that culminated in the true flowering of medieval aesthetics: the so-called Higashiyama culture.

This refined and far-reaching cultural movement takes its name from another Ashikaga residence: the villa built in the Higashiyama district of Kyoto by Yoshimitsu's grandson Yoshimasa (1435–90). Like his grandfather, Yoshimasa began the building of his retreat late in life, some eighty years after the completion of the Golden Pavilion. He devoted his whole spirit to the creation of what he hoped would be an ideal realm of beauty.

Although he was a man of the highest education, great taste, and subtle culture, Yoshimasa suffered a series of tragic disappointments and defeats in his

61. Pond in garden of Silver Pavilion, Jisho-ji, Kyoto.

career as shogun. Unlike his less restrained and more magnificent grandfather, he was a man of exquisite refinement. At the request of his mother, Hino Shigeko, he patterned his Higashiyama villa on the garden of the Saiho-ji, as Yoshimitsu had done at the Kitayama villa. But the results of Yoshimasa's borrowings differed radically from those achieved by Yoshimitsu. This is true because Yoshimasa, believing that he must make every effort to study the garden and the buildings of the Saiho-ji, applied his profound education and artistic perception to attain a thoroughly sensitive understanding of the creative forms and spaces used by Muso Kokushi. Yoshimitsu, on the other hand, manifested his quite different personality by seeing in the Saiho-ji only superficial novelty and splendor and by reflecting these aspects in his shining Golden Pavilion and its surrounding garden.

It is uncertain whether the Silver Pavilion at Yoshimasa's Higashiyama villa was ever actually covered with silver foil. In any case, it is in every way a much more subdued building than its golden counterpart. Planning the pavilion as a two-story building was more than direct copying of the Ruri-den at the Saiho-ji, and the decision to do so arose from the general proportional composition and expression of the Higashiyama garden as a whole. If it is true, as I have already suggested, that the Ocha no I stone arrangement (Fig. 59) at the Higashiyama villa was copied from the one at the Saiho-ji, it reveals Yoshimasa's power to understand Muso's concepts of garden design. It also reveals his humility in the face of them.

After Yoshimasa's death in 1490, the Higashi-yama villa became the temple Jisho-ji. This is the name it bears today, although it is better known as the Ginkaku-ji, or Temple of the Silver Pavilion. Unfortunately, it was damaged during the century or so of civil strife that closed the Muromachi period (1336–1568). The buildings and the garden (Figs. 57, 61) have been much repaired during succeeding centuries. Two of the most conspicuous features of the garden, the white-sand elevations called the Silver Sand Sea and the Moon-facing Mound (Fig. 57), were not part of the garden as Yoshimasa planned it. They were constructed during the Edo period (1603–1868) to fill in the space when one of the temple buildings burned down. Nevertheless, the white truncated cone of the Moon-facing Mound, whose form is reminiscent of Mount Fuji, and the wavelike pattern of the lower and broader Silver Sand Sea are far from commonplace in their abstract beauty and appeal.

THE EMERGENCE OF THE SHOIN-STYLE GARDEN

The Saiho-ji garden is one of the two gardens that compose the foundation for Muso Soseki's fame as a landscape artist. The other is the garden of the Tenryu-ji in the Arashiyama district of Kyoto. In the thirteenth century the site of the Tenryu-ji had been occupied by the Kameyama Palace of the retired emperor Gosaga. It commands a beautiful view of Arashi-yama, the hill that lies across from it on the Oi River. In 1342, Ashikaga Takauji, founder of the Ashikaga shogunate, delegated Muso Soseki to establish a Zen temple on this land as an offering for the repose of the spirit of the emperor Godaigo.

Converting the emperor Gosaga's former *shinden*-style estate to a Zen temple involved considerable alteration in the garden. The abbot's residence of the Tenryu-ji, for example, commands a view of the hills across the pond on the southwest (Fig. 60). This is a clear reversal of the standard *shinden* plan, in which the pond is invariably on the south of the main building. But this departure is similar to others made in Zen temples, which did not follow established custom in placement and plan. The pond is small and lacks the customary central island. The focal point of the distant shore as seen from the abbot's quarters is a stone arrangement representing a waterfall (Figs. 13, 52). Directly below this arrangement is a bridge made of natural stone slabs (Fig. 12). Numerous pointed and rough stones placed in the water nearby create the mood of a deep mountain valley. The tension of the stones in this part of the garden recalls that of the dry-landscape garden at the Saiho-ji, and the arrangement displays the severity typical of Muso's garden designs. Although it is conceivable that the group of stones standing in the pond near the foot of the dry waterfall represent Mount Sumeru of the Buddhist universe, their resemblance to similar stones in the pond of the Motsu-ji (Fig. 30) suggests that they are perhaps an example of the persistence of the Heian-period tradition of standing stones. The name of the Tenryu-ji pond—Sogen no Ike—and those of the nine other sections into which Muso divided the garden derive from Zen classics, since he was eager to incorporate Zen teachings in his garden plans.

With the garden of the Tenryu-ji, the art of the Japanese garden takes a turn in the direction of a style later to become intimately associated with *shoin* architecture: the mainstream of Japanese residential design in the feudal period. In the older *shinden*-style garden, people went boating on the pond and stopped at various fixed positions. Although they did not stroll through the garden, they were definitely in it. At the Tenryu-ji, however, the garden and the pond are manifestly designed to be enjoyed from a seated position within the abbot's quarters. The pond is too small for boating, and the bridge in front of the dry waterfall is not intended for walking. A very important change has been made in the basic concept of garden design: the amusement function of older gardens has been abandoned, and the garden is now designed solely for static appreciation. It is more than a coincidence that the Japanese residence, at about the same time, was undergoing a change from the older *shinden* to the newer *shoin* style. Still, it remains difficult to explain how two gardens designed by Muso Soseki within so short a time could clearly reveal this basic transition.

CHAPTER FOUR

The World of the Dry-Landscape Garden

GARDENS FOR ZEN DISCIPLINE Muso Soseki attempted to give physical form to his Zen philosophy in the dry-landscape garden of the Saiho-ji and the dry-waterfall stone group in the garden of the Tenryu-ji. Such gardens are in themselves a means toward Zen self-examination, spiritual refinement, and ultimate enlightenment. They therefore belong to a dimension of creativity entirely different from that of gardens designed for pleasure or for the gratification of aesthetic tastes. Zen gardens are not created specifically to be shown to people, but viewers nonetheless sense something profoundly moving in them. The believer discovers in them a world of the Zen spirit. The modern person uninitiated in Zen thought can see in them an art form representing a crystallization of spiritual energy. In short, if art may be defined as an awareness of the psychological tension of mankind, the dry-landscape garden represents art of a very high level.

Zen priests of the Muromachi period tried various approaches to the design of stone gardens, and many of the products of their efforts exist today as famous examples of garden art. Not all of these men and their works, however, fell under the influence of Muso Soseki. Rather, since their gardens were regarded as a means toward Zen discipline, copying was no doubt strictly forbidden. Indeed, it is

because they represent expressions of individual worlds of thought that Zen stone gardens have preserved their fame over the centuries.

After the dry-landscape garden of the Saiho-ji, the next most important design in this style is the stone garden in front of the abbot's quarters at the Daisen-in (Figs. 34, 62, 73–75), a subtemple of the Kyoto temple Daitoku-ji. The Daisen-in was founded by the Zen priest Kogaku, and since the plaque attached to the ridgepole of the abbot's quarters states that the framework of that building was completed in 1513, it is likely that the garden was constructed around that time. According to temple tradition, the great painter, poet, and man of broad aesthetic knowledge and talent Soami (?–1525) designed this garden and painted a landscape on the sliding partitions of the central room in the abbot's quarters. Records from the Edo period credit Soami with a number of gardens, but since no definite proof of his design exists, it may be that this is only another of the many groundless art attributions that occur in the aesthetic history of the time. For instance, both Muso Soseki and the famous tea master and garden designer Kobori Enshu are named, without authentication, as the creators of a number of gardens. It is probable that the temple founder Kogaku designed the Daisen-in garden as a place for Zen

62. *Dry waterfall, garden of abbot's quarters, Daisen-in, Daitoku-ji, Kyoto.*

discipline. If this were not so, the stone arrangements would undoubtedly lack their almost awesome tension.

The site of the garden is a small space on the east side of the rooms in which Kogaku is said to have lived. From the edge of the veranda to the clay wall opposite it, there is a depth of no more than three meters (Fig. 73), yet the bold masses of stone are so skillfully placed that one senses neither excess nor deficiency. Examples of such startling skill are rare.

Because it is a representation of a concrete kind of scenery, this stone arrangement is easier to understand than the abstract design at the Saiho-ji. The stones and gravel represent a course of water first falling over a waterfall (Figs. 34, 62), then racing along a mountain riverbed, and finally

flowing into a broad river (Fig. 73). The unusual nature of the arrangement played an important part in the early fame of the garden, but perhaps still more vital to its popularity was its comprehensibility. By contrast, the dry-landscape garden at the Saiho-ji was much less well known.

As viewed from a seated position on the mats of the adjacent room in the abbot's quarters, the garden is arranged to lead the eye from left to right, or from north to south. In the north corner, two large standing stones represent the waterfall. From this point the imaginary water races southward along its narrow valley bed to flow finally into a broad expanse on the right where a large boat-shaped stone seems to float on the surface (Fig. 75). White gravel raked into wave patterns figuratively flows from the mountain region on the

63. Stone arrangements in garden attributed to Sesshu, Joei-ji, Yamaguchi City, Yamaguchi Prefecture.

left to the expanse on the right, where it is broken slightly by two conical gravel mounds (Fig. 74).

Although the water is imaginary, in the right section of the garden it broadens out into a symbolization of the limitless expanses of an ocean. The skill with which this vast natural scene is encompassed in a very small space deserves great admiration. It would be very difficult for anyone other than a person like Kogaku, who had attained enlightenment through severe Zen discipline, to create this kind of world of fantasy.

Another feature of the garden that requires special notice is the roofed corridorlike bridge crossing the middle of the stone-and-gravel composition (Fig. 73). Until only a few years ago, this bridge was not there. But reference to pictures of the garden dating from the Edo period and investigation of remnants of mortises in the architecture

enabled specialists to reconstruct it. No more than a few tens of centimeters wide, the bridge is nonetheless crossable. Designed in an unusual roofed style admired by Zen priests, it has a walled section pierced by a cusped window (*kato mado*) and is furnished with a built-in bench. Small but usable, the bridge cuts across the garden in a startlingly bold way. Although it is functional, its scale surpasses mere practicality to maintain harmony with the expressive world of the garden and, in fact, to become a positive creative element in the spatial composition.

The Joei-ji garden, located in the city of Yamaguchi in Yamaguchi Prefecture, is attributed to Sesshu, one of the greatest of all Japanese painters. Its distinctively creative arrangement of a central pond and a lawn studded with stone groups is still in a good state of preservation (Figs. 37, 63). Of

64. *Stone arrangements on shore of northern pond, Sento Imperial Palace garden, Kyoto.*

65 *(overleaf, left). Steppingstone paths in garden area* ▷
around residential buildings, Katsura villa, Kyoto.

66 *(overleaf, right). Steppingstone approach to south* ▷
side of Old Shoin, Katsura villa, Kyoto.

67, 68. Views of Pond of the Bathing Dragon from south shore (left) and north shore (right); Upper Garden, Shugaku-in villa, Kyoto.

69 *(overleaf, left). Moss, ferns, maples, and azaleas in vicinity of Maple Hill, Sento Imperial Palace garden, Kyoto.* ▷

70 *(overleaf, right). Stroll path in vicinity of Maple Hill, Sento Imperial Palace garden, Kyoto.* ▷

72. *Stone outcrops at Akiyoshidai, Yamaguchi Prefecture.*

the roughly ten gardens said to have been designed by Sesshu in the Yamaguchi area and in Kyushu, only the Joei-ji garden is in sufficiently good condition to warrant appreciation. But for none of the gardens, including that of the Joei-ji, is there definite proof that Sesshu did in fact design them.

Formerly called the Myoki-ji, the Joei-ji was founded by the Ouchi daimyo family, which was powerful in the Yamaguchi region during the Muromachi period. The Ouchi, who made every effort to establish in their fief a culture in no way inferior to that prevailing in Kyoto, were active temple builders, and it seems that the garden of the Joei-ji was once on a level of splendor com-

parable to that of the Saiho-ji and the Temple of the Golden Pavilion.

The Joei-ji garden, although it has a pond, can properly be discussed among dry-landscape gardens because it too is a garden in the tradition of the Zen sect. This lawn-and-pond garden, surrounded on three sides by hills, is the only part of the total plan that can still be seen today. It was known as the Inner Garden, and the neighboring hills, which were called the Outer Garden, had three ponds of their own. A waterfall connected the upper ponds with the one in the Inner Garden below. Since the designer entrusted with giving unified landscape form to the vast project planned

◁ 71. *Detail of residential buildings and garden showing steppingstones and stone-filled gutter, Katsura villa, Kyoto.*

by the Ouchi family needed no mean skill, it is not surprising that the design has been attributed to a man of Sesshu's caliber.

Beginning at the edge of the veranda of the main temple building, the lawn rises gently until it reaches the pond, which is on a level roughly the same as that of the floor of the room facing the garden. The design composition is based on the topography of the site. The skillful combination of lawn, numerous stone groups dotted throughout the area, and low pruned shrubbery (Fig. 63), results in a visual composition unusual in Japanese garden art. Each of the stone groups has a geographical name—for example, Mount Hyakujo and Mount Fuji—and the garden itself is intended to be a representation of the whole world. The stone groups in the pond are named for the mythical Isles of the Blest: Horai, Eishu, and so on. Though it has now begun to crumble slightly, the

dry-waterfall stone group in the right background of the garden still suggests the powerful image of water that it must have suggested in times gone by.

Although people have come to accept the distinctive groupings of stones in this garden as original with Sesshu, it is probable that he derived the idea from the strikingly unusual landscape at Akiyoshidai in Yamaguchi Prefecture (Fig. 72), where grayish-white stone outcrops dot an upland meadow. Perhaps, after seeing this remarkable sight, Sesshu (if in fact he did design the garden) kept it in the back of his mind to bring forward later as an artistic representation of the great world in terms of a landscape garden.

The Taizo-in is a subtemple in the compound of the Zen temple Myoshin-ji in Kyoto. In temple tradition its dry-landscape garden (Figs. 38, 77, 100) is attributed to Kano Motonobu (1476–1559), one of the founders of the long-lived and prestigious

73. *Dry-landscape garden, abbot's quarters, Daisen-in, Daitoku-ji, Kyoto.*

Kano school of painters. This attribution is within reason because the garden is skillfully laid out for the sake of a view in a style at once reminiscent of Kano paintings and less profoundly influenced by the painting style of the Chinese Northern Sung dynasty than are the dry-landscape compositions at the Saiho-ji and the Daisen-in. Whether Moto-nobu designed it may be doubtful, but at any rate the psychological intent behind the garden is more consciously formalistic and ornamental than the designs of Muso Soseki and Kogaku. Although its stone arrangements are less breathtaking than Muso's arrangement in the Saiho-ji garden, within its limits the Taizo-in garden is an example of the skillful selection and placement of stones.

At the Reiun-in, also a subtemple of the Myo-shin-ji, there remains a small *shoin*-style building where the emperor Gonara is said to have practiced Zen discipline. Adjacent to it is a very small

but outstanding Muromachi-period dry-landscape garden said to have been designed by Shiken, a pupil of the famous painter Sesshu (Figs. 40, 76). A few carefully placed stones and some camellias and other plants arranged in a very small plot blend wonderfully with the subtle and compact *shoin* building to produce a space suitable for Zen study and training. Although the rooms in the building are small, they are outfitted with elaborately ornamented sliding entrance panels and were especially suited to the ceremonial needs of such highly placed personages as emperors and shoguns. Because of its elevated floor level and its delicate proportions the building has a special elegance. In all likelihood only a Zen priest of lofty spirit and advanced training and experience could provide a garden to harmonize with the graceful dignity of a building in such a small space. The composition of the garden at the Reiun-in

74. *Fish-eye view of raked-gravel patterns in dry-landscape garden, abbot's quarters, Daisen-in, Daitoku-ji, Kyoto.*

displays a sharp severity not to be found in the works of professional garden designers.

Among Zen stone gardens, the garden of the Ryoan-ji (Figs. 31, 78, 79), also in Kyoto, is on a level of excellence with that of the Daisen-in. Here, in a spread of carefully raked fine white gravel in front of the abbot's quarters, fifteen stones are placed in several groups of two and three. The beautiful balance of the garden appeals to the viewer in such a complex way that he never tires of looking at it. In fact, no similar garden has inspired as much wonder and admiration as this one. Some people invariably recall the medieval mood of the rough-surfaced stones, while others remember the more modern mood of the raked white gravel in which they stand. But for everyone the garden has an eternally new charm that is intensified by the mystery surrounding its creation. No one can say for certain when it was constructed or who designed it.

The Ryoan-ji was once the site of a villa owned by Tokudaiji Saneyoshi, a prominent figure in twelfth-century Japan. In the fifteenth century the property was acquired by the military leader Hosokawa Katsumoto, who converted it into a Zen temple. Toward the end of that century, after the disastrous Onin War of 1467–77, the abbot's residence was built. Other buildings were added and old ones renovated. Although there are no records to prove it, it is probable that the garden was constructed at this time.

Even if the garden dates from the late fifteenth century, it differed radically from the treeless, grassless composition that we see today, for in all likelihood the center of the visual appeal of the original plan was a group of magnificent cherry trees. It is reported that in the late sixteenth century the military dictator Toyotomi Hideyoshi visited the Ryoan-ji to view the cherry blossoms and to write poetry. As a result of his visit, one famous

75. *Stone arrangement in dry-landscape garden, abbot's quarters, Daisen-in, Daitoku-ji, Kyoto.*

76. *Dry-landscape garden and detail of* shoin *building, Reiun-in, Myoshin-ji, Kyoto.*

77. *Dry-landscape garden attributed to Kano Motonobu, Taizo-in, Myoshin-ji, Kyoto.*

tree, known as Hideyoshi's Cherry Tree, became the major attraction of the garden. The remains of this tree are still to be seen in the northwest corner of the garden in a spot where they do not seriously affect the composition. Since records calling special attention to the interest of the stones do not appear until the early seventeenth century, we can surmise that until then the cherry trees were the focal point of the composition and that the stones were only a contributing element. After the trees died, perhaps someone, discovering the interest of the stone groups themselves, built the enclosing clay-and-tile walls on the south and the west, eliminated all plants from the garden except the moss growing around the stones, and thus concentrated interest on the stones and the spread of white gravel.

If this is in fact what happened, the present appearance of the garden differs entirely from what the original designer intended. Nonetheless, his spirit and artistic ability must have been great indeed to have produced a garden that is not merely still worthy of appreciation but also fresh and beautiful even after it has been reduced to nothing but stones and gravel. In other words, his design for the placement of the stones went far beyond what would have been required of mere adjuncts to the cherry trees. His ability reveals such a lofty spiritual sophistication that he can only have been a Zen priest of great learning and virtue.

NEW TRENDS IN GARDEN DESIGN Until the time of the Reiun-in and the Ryoan-ji gardens, landscape compositions consisting of stones set in perfectly flat plots of ground had not existed. The majority of garden plans had made use of the topography of the bases of hills and

had employed rather large ponds as central features. Even very small gardens, like those of the Daisen-in and the Taizo-in, expressed the mood of mountain streams by means of varying levels. By contrast, the small Reiun-in garden is flat, and the only variation in levels is found among the stones themselves and in the different heights of the trees. The ideas represented in its design proved to be revolutionary in the history of gardens. Although these ideas were probably influenced by Chinese gardens or Chinese painting, they were essentially a new expression born of the refined aesthetic spirit of the previously noted Higashiyama culture.

This trend in design was not the creation of any individual garden designer. Instead, it was developed by a group of men representing the Zen-inspired cultural and aesthetic spirit that prevailed among cultivated people in the period of transition between the medieval and the early modern ages of Japanese history, and it enjoyed sufficient universality to become one of the main currents of later Japanese garden history.

At the Shinju-an subtemple of the Daitoku-ji is a stone garden traditionally said to have been designed by Murata Juko (1423–1502), reputed founder of the "rustic" style of the tea ceremony. The Shinju-an, it should be noted, is famous in Japan for its associations with the great Zen priest and poet Ikkyu (1394–1481).

The garden, which lies on the east side of the abbot's quarters, is a long, narrow, rectangular plot that widens slightly at its northern end (Figs. 39, 80–82). This limited area is completely covered with moss and set with a number of stone arrangements. The subtle and unpretentious placement of these stone groups, which gives them the natural

78. Dry-landscape garden, Ryoan-ji, Kyoto.

look of having been there for thousands of years, makes it quite reasonable to assume that tradition is correct in attributing the design of the garden to Juko.

A low clipped hedge runs along the border of the garden. The stones themselves suggest either mountains or islands in a sea of moss, but apart from the associations they evoke, their general style is at once restrained, distinctive, and individual. In the past, the distant mountains were visible beyond the low hedge, but today they are obscured by trees and houses. In other words, the garden is an early example of the borrowed-scenery technique, and it may have been because the design focused attention on the distant mountains that the stones are placed with such restraint. Since the borrowed-scenery technique—a development of the flat dry-landscape garden—did not come into

wide use until the seventeenth century, when the great designer Kobori Enshu was active, it may be correct to date the present Shinju-an garden from the early 1600's, when the abbot's residence was rebuilt. But no matter what the actual date may be, the garden deserves attention for the beauty of its combination of moss and stones in a flat plot.

In the dry-landscape gardens designed for flat plots of land, emphasis shifts from representational re-creations of natural scenery to compositions of abstract proportion and balance. In other words, even when standing stones represent waterfalls and flat stones represent bridges, the major intention of the plan is no longer realistic expression of the world of nature. Instead, the designer strives for formal beauty created by the shapes and sizes of plants and stones and by the balance and contrast among these elements. It is true that many abstract

79. *Detail of dry-landscape garden, Ryoan-ji, Kyoto.*

80. *Steppingstone approach and entrance gate, Shinju-an, Daitoku-ji, Kyoto.*

gardens treat certain topics allegorically: Mount Sumeru and the Buddhist cosmos, the mythical Isles of the Blest, Chinese ideas surrounding the concept of *yang* and *yin* (opposing positive and negative forces), the tortoise and the crane (traditional symbols of long life and good fortune), and simple mathematical combinations of seven, five, and three. But in most cases these elements are no more than names or expedient explanations tacked on to the garden features in later times, and they by no means always fit the essential forms of the gardens themselves. For instance, the seven-five-three compositional idea is often called in to explain the Shinju-an garden, and an elaborate tale of a tigress protecting her young from a demon is used to give narrative meaning to the Ryoan-ji garden, when in fact neither of these explanations is entirely apt. In spite of all these tacked-on theories and allegories, however, one can already see in these gardens the conscious application of modern compositional art for the sake of appreciation and enjoyment. The aesthetic theory behind this trend has much in common with the present-day tendency to produce the works of art known as *objets*.

This spirit of aesthetic form was the moving power behind the rapid development of modern Japanese art. Although the resulting greater freedom of form and layout was originally evolved for the sake of Zen temple gardens, it gradually penetrated to landscaping for private residences, which were themselves in a stage of transition from the

81. *Dry-landscape garden attributed to Murata Juko, abbot's quarters, Shinju-an, Daitoku-ji, Kyoto.*

older *shinden* to the newer *shoin* style. Inevitably, in connection with this shift in garden philosophy, the planning and designing of gardens passed from the hands of Zen priests into those of artist-designers, the earliest and one of the greatest of whom was Kobori Enshu (1579–1647).

Among the gardens whose design is attributed to Enshu is the famous one in front of the abbot's quarters at the Konchi-in, a subtemple of the great Zen monastery Nanzen-ji in Kyoto (Figs. 41, 85). South of an expanse of raked white gravel is an earthen bank completely concealed by clipped shrubbery. At the foot of the bank is a large central flat stone flanked on the left and the right by stone-group representations of the crane and the tortoise of auspicious association. Across the northwest corner of the gravel area stretches a line

of square, dressed steppingstones in an arrangement that is more ornamental than is usual in the Zen garden (Fig. 41).

The garden of the abbot's residence at the Daitoku-ji, also attributed to Enshu, consists of a south section and a long, narrow east section that joins it at right angles (Figs. 3–5, 33). At the southeast corner, the point of juncture, stands a *sanzon* (Buddhist triad) stone group that resembles a waterfall arrangement (Fig. 5). On either side of this group are other stone groups, trees, and low-growing plants. The entire composition is executed with great skill. In addition the garden employs the borrowed-scenery technique, offering a view of Mount Hiei and Mount Daimonji across a low, straight hedge on the east side (Fig. 4). Perhaps the most subtle refinement in the garden is the

82. Stone group in garden of abbot's quarters, Shinju-an, Daitoku-ji, Kyoto.

balance maintained between the visually emphasized eastern section and the expanse of white gravel and stones in its northwest corner.

For the deliberate and complete calculation of all these visual effects and for the realization of the plan in concrete terms through the employment of a variety of techniques, the genius of a man like Kobori Enshu was essential. But this is not all that was needed. Without a social basis to support the general diffusion of this formal art, the modern garden could not have come into being. In feeling, these gardens differ essentially from the spirit represented by the works of Muso Soseki, but the effect of the new trend was not wholly salutary, for this garden philosophy was fated to include a danger of lapsing into imitation, vulgarization, and formalization.

In Bofu, Yamaguchi Prefecture, is a famous stone garden known as the Tsuki no Katsura garden (Figs. 8, 83, 84). Although nothing definite is known about its historical period or its designer, a tradition of the Katsura family holds that it was built in the eighteenth century, when a certain Katsura Tadaharu renovated the *shoin* residence to which it is adjacent. This garden, like the one at the abbot's quarters of the Daitoku-ji, consists of south and east sections that join at right angles (Fig. 84). It is enclosed by a tile-topped clay wall and is entirely spread with raked gravel in which large and small stones of rather unusual shapes have been placed (Fig. 8). Some of the stones bear such appellations as Clam and Rabbit.

The garden is unusual for a regional district far removed from the sphere of the cultural centers of

83. *Stone arrangement in Tsuki no Katsura garden, Bofu, Yamaguchi Prefecture.*

84. *Fish-eye view of Tsuki no Katsura dry-landscape garden, Bofu, Yamaguchi Prefecture.*

85. Garden of abbot's quarters, Konchi-in, Nanzen-ji, Kyoto.

its time. The stones, said to have come from the nearby hills, produce a rougher and stronger effect than the ones generally used in the gardens of Kyoto. As the large L-shaped stone perched on a smaller stone (Fig. 83) indicates, the grouping method is extravagant and suggests that the designer was a man of boldness and courage. Katsura Tadaharu, for whom the garden is supposed to have been constructed, was a samurai, a Zen adept, a poet, and the founder of a school of the tea ceremony. It is therefore quite likely that he designed the garden himself, for only a man of his cultivation and spirit could have created a design as untrammeled by tradition as this one.

Furuta Oribe, one of the most important followers of the great tea master Sen no Rikyu (1521–91), is said to have designed the stone garden of the Nanshu-ji in Sakai, Osaka Prefecture (Fig. 99). As a samurai tea master with a very individual aesthetic of tea, Oribe designed a number of tea gardens, although none of them are extant today. Nevertheless, the Nanshu-ji garden suggests what his garden style may have been like.

Somewhat showy for a Zen temple, the garden design employs the colors and shapes of stones in a composition that seems to overflow with a spirit of modernity. One of its striking features is an imaginary stream that emerges from under a stone bridge and describes a vigorous line through the setting. Whether Oribe actually designed the garden or not, these features are characteristic of his taste.

CHAPTER FIVE

Gardens of the Late Feudal and the Early Modern Periods

THE SHOIN-STYLE GARDEN OF THE MOMOYAMA PERIOD

As we look back over the changing social status of the garden designer, we can trace an interesting course of development. In the Heian period the court nobles and aristocrats themselves, by directing the designs and plans of their own gardens along lines that reflected their education and tastes, made great contributions to the advancement of garden art. Then, as gardens constructed for temples of the Jodo sect increased in number, Buddhist priests assumed a leading role in one area of design and thereby added their religious knowledge to the store of garden philosophy. Naturally, out of the large number of priests engaged in such work, certain especially talented men emerged to make garden design their major concern. These men came to be known as *sekiritsu so,* or stone-arranging priests. Most of the pond and stone gardens constructed for temples during the Kamakura period (1185–1336) were the products of their skills. The majority of these stone-arranging priests belonged to the Shingon sect of Buddhism, and, among them, priests from the Ninna-ji temple in Kyoto were notable for their activities.

During the Muromachi period, Zen Buddhism became a major religious force, and, with the emergence of the great priest Muso Soseki, a revolution in gardening styles occurred. Throughout this age, learned priests and other people of culture refined garden making and gradually developed it into an art primarily concerned with the aesthetic appreciation of form. It is true that garden making during this period became a kind of occupation, many of whose workers were looked upon with a certain opprobrium. On the other hand, some garden designers were men of genius associated with the lofty circles of the shoguns themselves. For instance, Zen'ami, a man of extensive artistic talents, enjoyed the patronage of the Ashikaga shogun Yoshimasa and, in addition to his other cultural activities, participated in some of the most outstanding garden-design projects of the fifteenth century. His son Kojiro and his grandson Matajiro are also recorded as having been talented garden designers.

After almost a century of civil strife that began in the middle years of the Muromachi period, the military dictator Toyotomi Hideyoshi (1536–98) brought unity to a divided and war-torn Japan and thereby ushered in the late feudal period, which lasted until 1868. The age in which he flourished was the Momoyama period (1568–1603), which took its name from the hill called Momoyama, site of his Fushimi Castle in Kyoto. The stability he established gave rise to an extravagant

86. Detail of garden showing stone arrangements and clipped shrubbery, Sambo-in, Daigo-ji, Kyoto.

upsurge of building and rebuilding projects. Hideyoshi, whose tastes inclined toward the gorgeous and the magnificent, built a number of splendid residences and castles for his own use, among them the castle-palace Juraku-dai, the above-mentioned Fushimi Castle, and Osaka Castle. In addition to having a passion for architecture, he was deeply interested in gardens, and he naturally surrounded his dazzling structures with landscaping of great beauty. Unfortunately, none of his imposing buildings and their gardens survive today, but it is still possible to learn, from the garden at the Sambo-in subtemple of the Daigo-ji in Kyoto (Figs. 86, 87, 105), something about his aesthetic propensities and the wealth that supported them. Hideyoshi is said to have planned the garden and directed its construction shortly before his death in 1598.

We are told that Hideyoshi, in preparation for giving an elaborate cherry-blossom party, made an inspection tour of this part of the Daigo-ji (the Sambo-in was then called the Kongorin-in) and, finding the site to his taste, ordered large-scale reconstruction. He died before his plans were carried out, but Gien Jugo, the abbot of the temple, saw the work through in accordance with Hideyoshi's wishes. The project ultimately required twenty-eight years for its completion.

So great had been Hideyoshi's own expectations of the Sambo-in and its garden that he had had a famous stone—the so-called Fujito Stone—removed from his Juraku-dai castle-palace and placed there. Nor was Gien less enthusiastic. From the garden workers available at the time, he selected only the best for the project. He had the waterfall arrangement, which Hideyoshi himself had specified, rebuilt a number of times and was not entirely satisfied until he had obtained the services of a certain Kentei, who was famous as a garden designer

87. *Detail of garden showing stone arrangements and pond, Sambo-in, Daigo-ji, Kyoto.*

88. *Kasa-tei teahouse and approach, Kozan-ji, Kyoto.* ▷

and whose name meant "excellent gardener."

The building facing the garden is called the Front Shoin, since it is designed in the *shoin* residential style employed for the mansions of the feudal-period warrior class. Its sliding paper-and-wood partitions are decorated with paintings by members of the prestigious Kano school in the showy style of the Momoyama period. But certain other aspects of the building reveal Hideyoshi's respect for things more subtle and aristocratic. For example, the veranda that integrates interior space with that of the garden is open in the manner of the *shinden*-style mansions of court nobles in earlier times. In addition, a section of the building, known as the Izumi-dono, projects into the garden in a fashion reminiscent of the fishing pavilions common to *shinden*-style buildings (Fig. 86).

THE PERFECTION OF THE EARLY MODERN GARDEN

Hideyoshi's fondness for the rich and the colorful gave birth to the Momoyama culture, which, like the period itself, took its name from the site of his Fushimi Castle. At the same time it produced a reaction against ostentatious display and thereby stimulated the growth of the diametrically opposed movement represented by the restraint, refinement, and elegant simplicity of the tea ceremony. In fact, it was the combination of Hideyoshi and the great tea master Sen no Rikyu, his aesthetic adviser, that provided the force to determine the direction in which early modern Japanese culture developed. If the glory of Momoyama taste is compared to brilliant light, then the somber profundities of Rikyu's aesthetics are the gentle gloom that gave

depth to modern art and added to it a sense of multilevel meaning. To use another simile, if I may compare these two trends to the two parts of the Saiho-ji garden, Hideyoshi's predilections and the art they inspired may be likened to the resplendent and now vanished pavilion called the Ruri-den; Rikyu's cult of tea, to the dry-landscape arrangement in the upper garden. Whereas the lost pavilion was an expression of physical, almost carnal, pleasure, Rikyu's genius gave medieval severity richer expression in the form of the tea ceremony, which introduced art into daily life and, in time, led to the spatial unity between interior and exterior found in teahouses and tea gardens and ultimately in all buildings and gardens in the *sukiya*, or teahouse, style.

At the Tai-an of the Myoki-an and the Kasa-tei (Fig. 88) and the Shigure-tei of the Kodai-ji (all in Kyoto), it is possible to see traces of designs of teahouses and tea gardens by Rikyu. Even in their greatly diminished forms, these hints of past beauties reveal the great power of his influence. It was indeed this influence that marked an epoch in the history of Japanese architecture and garden art. Rikyu's aesthetic force extended beyond teahouses and tea gardens to reach general residential gardens and, even more important, to propagate among the Japanese people a new artistic awareness and a different kind of expression through artistic forms.

As an example of the beauty of spatial arrangements resulting from a blend of architecture and garden, the Katsura villa (or Katsura Detached Palace) is without peer (Figs. 65, 66, 71, 89–93, 103, 130–32, 134, 135, 147–49, 152, 156, 158). It

89. *Stone-paved walk and steppingstones at entrance to Old Shoin, Katsura villa, Kyoto.*

is a crystallization of the aesthetic consciousness of the imperial family and the court aristocracy combined with the appreciation of beauty represented by the entire *sukiya* tradition. During the more than two centuries of feudal society that remained after Katsura was built, nothing was produced to surpass the loveliness of its spaces.

In the first half of the seventeenth century the Tokugawa shogunate finally succeeded in establishing itself firmly in power over a unified Japan. It was during this time that the Katsura villa was built in stages by the imperial prince Hachijo no Miya Toshihito and his son Noritada. This was also the age when the great aesthetician and tea master Kobori Enshu was displaying unparalleled genius in a number of building and garden-design projects. Although a long-popular story attributes the design of the Katsura garden to Enshu, no direct connection with him has ever been proved. Nevertheless, the influence of the novel creativity he revealed in numerous other gardens can be traced in both tangible and intangible elements of the Katsura design.

The garden occupies more than 40,000 square meters on the shore of the Katsura River in Kyoto. The residential buildings consist of three connected sections: the Old Shoin (Fig. 90), the Middle Shoin, and the New Palace. Each section was built at a different time, and all are arranged in a staggered line. The front section of the Old Shoin faces a large pond (Fig. 90). Paths for strolling lead around the pond and to several teahouses, including the Shokin-tei (Figs. 92, 103) and the Shoi-ken (Fig. 93), and some smaller waiting pavilions. The entire plan of the garden is extremely free. It represents a blend of the austerity of the world of tea and the expansiveness of the *shinden* mansions of the Heian-period aristocracy. A sense of strong formal control and refined technique pervades the whole layout.

Enough has already been said in countless other books about the elegance, restraint, and subdued beauty of the staggered placement of components, the white walls, the unfinished wooden structural members, and the cypress-bark-shingle roof of the main residential structure (Fig. 71). The sense of rapport between this *sukiya*-style elegance and the

90. Old Shoin and pond, Katsura villa, Kyoto.

92. Shokin-tei teahouse, stone arrange- ▷
ments, and pond, Katsura villa, Kyoto.

rusticity of the darkened wood and thatched roofs of the teahouses across the pond from the residence is so deeply lyrical and moving that words cannot express the feeling that all visitors to Katsura experience. I should like to say, however, that I find the key to the incomparable beauty of Katsura in the skillful working out of the various approaches.

First of all, the movement lines throughout the composition are planned to present the viewer with constantly altering vistas as the paths lead from the river to the main gate, from there to the Miyukimon (the gate reserved for use by members of the imperial family), to the front entrance of the residence, and then around the pond so as to connect each of the large and small buildings. The amazingly compact unity of the design, in spite of the flux and halt of the movement lines, represents the epitome of

an almost magical skill in garden design. Again, many elements related to the approaches—the hedge of woven bamboo (Fig. 134), the bamboo-and-brushwood fence (Fig. 135), the paving of small flat stones on the walk that leads from the Miyukimon to the inner gate (Fig. 91)—conceal astounding creative skill in an apparently casual expression.

The paths in tea-garden style that lead around the main building and connect the teahouses and waiting pavilions form a composition that symbolizes the world of the tea ceremony. Within this tranquil harmony the paths are enlivened for the visitor by dramatic changes of mood and scene. For instance, in some places the steppingstones, each selected so that its shape suits the topography, describe multidimensional arcs that are abruptly

broken by means of the forceful straight lines of cut-stone pavement leading to a ritual water basin or a waiting pavilion. Sometimes the paths lead from gravel-spread areas or luxuriant beds of moss to the pounded-earth areas under the eaves of a building or to a boat landing at the edge of the pond. In taking their various directions and presenting their various views, they suggest a virtually limitless continuity. This free and generous guidance from place to place in the garden, together with the preservation of suitable intervals between the scenic highlights, is calculated with startling ingenuity in everything from small details to the total spatial plan. The tremendous creative energy required for a design of this kind could only have originated in the fortunate combination of two elements: first, the knowledge of a group of mature

craftsmen well acquainted with old traditions and new techniques and, second, the education and sensitivity of the Hachijo princes, who knew how to make maximum use of the talents of their workers.

The celebrated garden of the Shugaku-in villa (or Shugaku-in Detached Palace, as it is officially called), almost contemporary in construction with the Katsura villa and garden and a masterpiece in its own right, was created for the retired emperor Gomizuno-o (Figs. 2, 6, 7, 36, 67, 68, 106, 107, 136). Gomizuno-o, a nephew of Prince Toshihito, who began the building of Katsura, often visited the prince there. The relationship between the men was more than just a family one, for Gomizuno-o received instruction from his uncle in ancient and modern culture. As a result, it is scarcely

93. *Under-eaves area, Shoi-ken teahouse, Katsura villa, Kyoto.*

surprising that the spirit of the Katsura garden should manifest itself at Shugaku-in, even though in physical form and artistic expression the two gardens are quite different. Perhaps the most notable point of difference is found in the Shugaku-in Upper Garden (Kami no Chaya), which centers on a vast artificial pond surrounded by extensive stretches of clipped shrubbery. The composition of the Upper Garden, employing the borrowed-scenery technique, embraces a panoramic view of distant hills and mountains as well as a view of the city of Kyoto (Figs. 2, 36, 67, 68). There is little here to suggest the delicate *sukiya* tastes of Katsura, and possibly the life and experiences of Gomizuno-o explain this approach to garden design. He had been bitterly disappointed and ultimately defeated in several political conflicts with the all-powerful Tokugawa shogunate, and it may have been that he chose this kind of garden in the hope of escaping from the world of political turmoil by submerging himself in an engulfing and splendid nature.

Even though the Katsura and the Shugaku-in gardens both feature ponds and paths for strolling, the ideas behind their physical designs have almost nothing in common. For instance, in contrast with the subtle variations and modulations of the Katsura design, at Shugaku-in the path along the top of the dike that retains the pond follows a perfectly straight line (Figs. 7, 36). In addition, the large curving slope of clipped shrubbery lying between the Rin'un-tei pavilion and the pond (Fig. 6) strictly rejects all variations in the pattern of its surface. More important than these differences,

94. *Pond and stone dike, Korakuen Park, Tokyo.*

95. *View of garden and pond, Rikugien Park, Tokyo.*

96. *View of garden showing lawn-covered artificial hills, with stone water basin in foreground, Suizenji Park, Kumamoto City, Kumamoto Prefecture.*

97. *View of garden and borrowed scenery (Mount Hiei), abbot's quarters, Shoden-ji, Kyoto.*

98. *View of garden from main room, Jiko-in, Yamato Koriyama, Nara Prefecture.*

99. *Dry-landscape garden attributed to Furuta Oribe, Nanshu-ji, Sakai, Osaka Prefecture.*

100. Stone arrangement in dry-landscape garden attributed to Kano Motonobu, Taizo-in, Myoshin-ji, Kyoto.

102. *Boat landing, northern pond, Sento Imperial Palace garden, Kyoto.*

◁ 101. *Cobblestone beach, southern pond, Sento Imperial Palace garden, Kyoto.*

103. *View of garden pond and Shokin-tei teahouse, Katsura villa, Kyoto.*

104. Pond, stone arrangements, and stone bridge in garden of Ninomaru compound, Nijo Castle, Kyoto.

106. *Jugetsu-kan, Lower Garden (Shimo no Chaya), Shugaku-in villa, Kyoto.*

however, is the distinction between the aims of the two gardens. Whereas the Katsura garden strives to direct the attention of the viewer inward, the Upper Garden of Shugaku-in is deliberately planned to melt, so to speak, into the distant scenery of mountains and plains for the sake of an expansive, outgoing mood.

Originally the Shugaku-in villa consisted of the Upper Garden and the Lower Garden, the latter of which centers on an attractive stream and the teahouse called the Jugetsu-kan (Fig. 106). Later a third section, called the Middle Garden (Fig. 107), was added as a setting for the building known as the Rakushi-ken, which then became part of the residence of Gomizuno-o's eighth daughter. In the Lower Garden, the area in front of the Jugetsu-kan

is spread with white gravel set with steppingstones. Nearby is a stone arrangement with a waterfall. The garden preserves a deep tranquility that suggests the Zen-oriented tastes of the retired emperor. Although the Middle Garden today has a somewhat desolate air, the pond and its surroundings in front of the Rakushi-ken (Fig. 107) are still quite feminine in mood.

The Sento Imperial Palace in Kyoto, official residence of the retired emperor Gomizuno-o, was built before Shugaku-in. Work on the palace and its garden (Figs. 64, 69, 70, 101, 102, 108, 109, 154) was begun in 1628, but the plan was altered many times in later years. The palace has been burned, rebuilt, and remodeled on three different occasions during its history. Although Kobori

◁ *105. Stone arrangements, pond, and waterfall, Sambo-in garden, Daigo-ji, Kyoto.*

107. *View of Middle Garden (Naka no Chaya), Shugaku-in villa, Kyoto.*

Enshu designed the original garden, frequent changes have left only a few parts of the design to attest to his skill. Nevertheless, since first-rate garden designers were employed in all the reconstructions and alterations—as is only to be expected in the case of an imperial property—the Sento Palace garden today preserves an elegance and a beauty that entitle it to be called a masterpiece of its kind.

A spacious rectangular plot, long in the north-south axis, the Sento Palace garden has two ponds, one in the northern part and one in the southern. The garden is designed for strolling, and the moods of the areas around the two ponds contrast sharply. The shore of the northern pond is bright and serene, and gently curving stretches of lawn contribute to this mood (Figs. 64, 102, 109). The major feature of the southern section, on the other hand,

is a stretch of beach completely covered with carefully selected cobblestones (Fig. 101). The differences in nature between the two parts of the garden derive from the original division of the present plot into a northern half, containing the residence of the cloistered empress Tofukumon-in, and the southern half, which contained the residence of the retired emperor Gomizuno-o. The two halves of the plot were combined into a single garden in a reconstruction carried out during the eighteenth century.

Between the two major sections a strolling path gently winds around the base of a hillock covered with maple trees (Figs. 69, 70) and smooth lawns. The mood in this part of the garden suggests complete security and a gentleness not often found in garden plans. Although this linking area may have been produced when the two former gardens were

108. *Peninsula and shoreline stone arrangements in southern pond, Sento Imperial Palace garden, Kyoto.*

joined, the indefinite nature of its general atmosphere was probably not accidental.

The northern section, popularly called the Lawn Garden, skillfully employs expanses of grass to create a feminine feeling suitable to the residence of a former empress living a life of retirement. But even more impressive is the mastery with which stones are used to highlight the lawns (Fig. 64). This is especially true of the handsome stones placed beside the garden paths. A curved stone bridge crosses the pond at a point where a spring is said to have existed in former times (Fig. 109). This bridge and a straight cut-stone retaining wall near the boat landing in the southwestern part of the garden give a special accent to their setting and thus enhance the elegance of the total plan.

Each of the cobblestones that cover the beach in the south garden is in itself an attractive object,

but the feat of amassing enough of them to pave so large an area is quite astounding. The shoreline itself could hardly be more beautiful.

The parts of the garden that are said to preserve the original design of Kobori Enshu are the cut-stone retaining wall at the eastern side of the south pond, the stone groups edging the peninsula that juts into this pond (Fig. 108), and the boat landing in the southeast corner of the north pond (Fig. 154). It is certain that the sharp incline of the stone steps at this boat landing suggests the formal boldness that one might expect of Enshu.

GARDENS OF MIL- The opening of the late
ITARY RULERS feudal period was preceded
by a long age of internal strife. Japanese castles, which represent one of the pinnacles of feudal-period architecture, were natu-

109. Stroll path and stone arrangements on shore of northern pond, Sento Imperial Palace garden, Kyoto.

*110. View of garden, Ninomaru compound,
Nijo Castle, Kyoto.*

*111. Stone arrangements and pond, Ninomaru
compound, Nijo Castle, Kyoto.*

112. Stone-covered area around north Noh stage, Nishi Hongan-ji, Kyoto.

rally born of the military requirements for guarding strategic locations. Later, however, when a strong government brought peace to Japan, these buildings came to symbolize the wealth and power of the military class. As a result of this development, the buildings increased in splendor and luxurious ornament. Vast amounts of labor and money went into the creation of an unparalleled type of architectural magnificence. All the features of the earlier Japanese castle—the gleaming, towering donjon, the forbidding moat and stone ramparts, and the glittering *shoin*-style residential buildings of the castle lord—represent the passion, the young blood, and the strength of a new age. As the feudal social order struck deeper roots and introduced greater political and economic stability, castle architecture and the gardens within castle compounds became more sedate and more profoundly expressive.

Edo Castle, now long since vanished and replaced on the same site by the Tokyo Imperial Palace, was the seat of power of the Tokugawa clan, which ruled Japan in peace for more than two and a half centuries. Although the stately and serene ramparts within the castle's inner moat (the only parts that survive today) may not be called a garden in the strictest sense, they could never have been built without the rich experience and creative talent on which all early modern Japanese gardens are based. Not only are they very gardenlike in feeling, but they can also be counted among the most beautiful and distinctly Japanese compositions in the whole country (Fig. 144).

Not enough remains of the gardens of Edo Castle to give an idea of their appearance at the height of their beauty, but the Ninomaru compound of Nijo Castle in Kyoto survives today as a

113. Stone bridge at gate to Koho-an, Daitoku-ji, Kyoto.

forceful and magnificent symbol of the ostentatious tastes of the Momoyama period. It is no exaggeration to say this, for the residential *shoin* buildings that face the garden are distinguished by some of the most gilded and glorious Momoyama-style interiors in Japan. The garden, which is supposed to have been designed by Kobori Enshu, employs vast numbers of stone groups to achieve a balance with the massive architecture (Figs. 104, 110, 111). In a most emphatic way it reveals the great distance that separated the gentle and quiet world of the men who designed and commissioned the Katsura and Sento Palace gardens and the vigorous world of the mighty daimyo who built and lived in the great castles of the age.

In splendor of Momoyama-period décor, the *shoin* buildings of the Kyoto temple Nishi Hongan-ji rival those of Nijo Castle. Standing among them

are two Noh stages, both reportedly transported there from Hideyoshi's Fushimi Castle. The area between the north Noh stage and the surrounding *shoin* buildings is spread with rough-textured black stones of oval shape, all carefully turned the same way so that they give the impression of a wave-washed, stone-paved beach (Fig. 112). In contrast with the calm effect produced by the cobblestone beach at the Sento Imperial Palace, this area at the Nishi Hongan-ji creates a vigorous Momoyama-style mood suited to the adjacent *shoin* buildings.

KOBORI ENSHU AND THE TEA GARDEN

When the long age of civil strife came to a close with the unification of Japan at the beginning of the seventeenth century, the ruling military leaders felt a pressing need to restore hope and glory to the nation by

114. *Detail of stone-paved approach to Koho-an, Daitoku-ji, Kyoto.*

embarking on a period of rapid and extensive reconstruction. The increased demand for planners and builders resulted in more orderly organization of the construction industry and in modernization of architectural techniques. Government-sponsored projects included such vast undertakings as the restoration of the Kyoto Imperial Palace, the building of the Sento Imperial Palace, the reconstruction of Osaka Castle, and the building of Nijo Castle, the last two of which served as residences for the shogun when he sojourned in Osaka or in Kyoto. To insure excellent work, the shogunate appointed qualified men to act as general chiefs in charge of these projects. Under each general chief were a number of shogunal administrators, each responsible for a number of foremen and their subordinates. The tightly organized design-

and-construction group was rounded out with as many carpenters and other workers as were required for the project in hand.

In 1606, Kobori Enshu received his first commission as an administrator of the building of a palace for the emperor Goyozei. This initial assignment was followed by numerous similar assignments that culminated in his appointment as general chief of the work on the inner compound of Nijo Castle, which was being extensively refurbished in preparation for an imperial visit to the shogun. Although this commission firmly established Enshu's fame, the originality and creativity of his work on numerous other projects was the basis on which his reputation rested.

Enshu Kobori Masaichi, to give him his original full name, was born in Omi Province in 1579. His

115. View of garden from Bosen tearoom, Koho-an, Daitoku-ji, Kyoto.

116. *Steppingstones and ritual water basin in tea garden, Fushin-an, Omote Senke school of tea, Kyoto.*

father, Shinsuke, had been chief retainer to Toyotomi Hidenaga, younger brother of Hideyoshi. This connection made it possible for young Enshu to study the tea ceremony with Sen no Rikyu, who was Hideyoshi's chief adviser on aesthetics. In addition, Enshu studied the art of tea with Furuta Oribe. At that time many of the warrior class were followers of Zen. Enshu's family was no exception, and he studied Zen precepts with Shun'oku Soen at the Daitoku-ji, where in later years he built his own Zen retreat, the Koho-an. Because of his deep knowledge of Zen and tea traditions, he was commissioned to supervise work on Zen temples and ordinary *sukiya*-style buildings in addition to that involving many official gardens and buildings.

It is important, however, to keep one thing in mind when discussing the manifold activities of this remarkable man: it was not his own talent alone that made him a virtual legend for amazing industry and genius in design. It would have been impossible for him to supervise the planning and actual construction of the almost countless and widely distributed gardens and buildings with which he is credited. He required and obtained a number of associates who understood and sympathized with his ideas. In addition, he enjoyed the use of the kind of tight construction organization noted above. Among the relatives who assisted him were his younger brother Masaharu, his nephew Gempei (Masaharu's son), and his nephew Kurobei. He was also assisted by such men as the chief retainer Kobori Genzaemon and another retainer, Murase Sasuke. These talented and cultivated men, as well as many highly skilled laborers

117. *Approach to Fushin-an teahouse, Omote Senke school of tea, Kyoto.*

118. View from Kikugetsu-tei pavilion, Ritsurin Park, Takamatsu, Kagawa Prefecture.

organized in efficient groups, contributed much to the successful completion of Enshu's undertakings. But ultimately it was because he knew how to use his helpers as if they were extensions of himself, and because his design philosophy was strong and vigorous, that gardens and buildings in the Enshu style could be created without his direct participation. It may be largely for this reason that innumerable designs—like that of the Katsura villa, for example—have been attributed without proof to the hands of this great artist.

The two extant works of garden design that can with greatest assurance be attributed to Enshu can be seen at the Koho-an subtemple of the Daitoku-ji. They are the garden of the Bosen tearoom and the stone pavement that leads from the front gate of the Koho-an to its main entrance. Both date

from the last years of this master of tea and Zen, and both represent the culmination of his concepts of tea-garden design. The original Bosen tearoom was also from his hand, but it no longer exists.

The stone pavement (Fig. 114) runs for a distance of some forty meters from the front gate and then turns at a right angle to lead to the main entrance and, beyond it, the service entrance. Its severe design creates a mood suitable to the world of the Zen temple. The skillful combination of long, rectangular dressed stones and stones in natural shape is so attractive that one forgets the length of the walk. Further variation in the pattern is attained by the occasional use of L-shaped stones or stones with one side cut to form a curve. The bridge leading from the street in front of the gate to the stone pavement harmonizes with the general com-

119. *Pond and pile-supported beaches, Rikugien Park, Tokyo.*

position (Fig. 113). In a typical Enshu design, carefully dressed stones in the bridge are juxtaposed with rough, angular natural stones on either side to reflect the forcefulness of the similar combination of paving stones beyond the gate.

Enshu's Bosen tearoom was destroyed by fire but was faithfully reconstructed in the eighteenth century, mainly through the efforts of Matsudaira Fumai, a devotee of the tea ceremony and a member of a powerful daimyo family. Its garden (Fig. 115) fully expresses the tea ceremony as Enshu interpreted it, and the building, although it is in the *shoin* style, displays great freedom in its spatial composition. In fact, this spatial composition, in which building and garden are united by means of a slightly lower veranda, is unique in its creative originality. Perhaps the most startlingly bold de-

parture in the design of the building is to be seen in the *shoji* panels that fill the upper half of the opening that faces the garden (Fig. 115). Unlike the usual *shoji*, which reach from floor to lintel, these sliding panels of translucent paper seem to be suspended in the air, and the open space below them most effectively integrates the garden with the interior of the room. At the same time the room is sheltered from the western sun. Although this treatment of the *shoji* is completely original, it remains just outside the limits of tea-ceremony rules. Nevertheless, it reveals the formal strength of Enshu's design and his deep refinement in both tea and Zen.

In may well be that the leading tea masters who succeeded Sen no Rikyu made the greatest contribution to the development of the subtle nuances

120. *Double-peaked artificial hill, Korakuen Park, Tokyo.*

and the complicated beauty that distinguish the modern Japanese garden. These men were mostly concerned with a style of garden called a *roji* (literally, "dewy path"), which is fundamentally a pathway leading from the garden gate to the teahouse. But because it is also essential for the *roji* to prepare the guest psychologically to enter the world of tea, its design and spatial expression require intense care. It must have a balanced sense of both flow and calm in its movement lines. Its mood must be tense in some places and relaxed in others, with a suitable equilibrium maintained between the two. All distracting elements must be eliminated, for they introduce jarring worldly thoughts. Over the centuries, tea masters have perfected a *roji* garden space that is an expression of the world of tea. In many repeated refinements these same men have also perfected superb tech-

niques of design to produce the required mood.

After the death of Sen no Rikyu in 1591, his son Shoan inherited his property in Kyoto and became head of the school of tea that had developed around his father's precepts. In the seventeenth century the property was divided into two sections, and these, in turn, became the headquarters of two different schools of tea: the Omote Senke (literally, "front Sen residence") and the Ura Senke (literally, "back Sen residence"). Both have continued for well over three centuries as major schools of the tea ceremony, and each has a celebrated garden furnished with various teahouses. Although all of the original buildings have been burned down and subsequently rebuilt, the steppingstones and ritual water basins remain to give a fairly faithful approximation of what the gardens looked like in the past. Figures 116, 117, 140, and 141 show features of the

121. View of Murin-an garden and villa, Kyoto.

Omote Senke garden, which centers on the Fushin-an teahouse.

Along the approach to the Fushin-an is a free-standing section of clay wall pierced by a low window through which the tea-ceremony guests pass by way of high steppingstones on either side (Fig. 141). This *naka-kuguri,* or window-gate, as it is called, simultaneously isolates the tea garden from the ordinary world and invites the visitor to step inside. The combined isolation-invitation mood is further expressed in the placement of the steppingstones that lead to and from the *naka-kuguri.* These stones are set in a deep bed of moss. It is said that the idea of the *naka-kuguri* originated with Sen no Rikyu himself.

As we have noted above, the tea garden must maintain a balance between moods of relaxation and tension. Such a balance is skillfully achieved at the Fushin-an. The steppingstones in front of the waiting pavilion seem to have been merely scattered across the small plot of ground in a setting of care-free and relaxing abandon (Fig. 140), but those leading to the teahouse itself restore a strict, all-pervading tension to the space (Fig. 117). The careful modulation and variation of moods found in the approach composition of tea gardens was used in many other gardens of the early modern period and may indeed be called the element that perfected the beauty of Japanese-style garden spaces.

THE STROLL GARDEN The Tokugawa feudal system, instituted at the beginning of the seventeenth century, brought stability to the warrior class and created a distinctive culture. At the peak of this late feudal society stood

122. Brook and pond, Murin-an garden, Kyoto.

the shogunal family. Just below them were the daimyo, or feudal lords, and subordinate to these were the samurai, less wealthy and less powerful. Each of these groups strove to evolve a culture suited to the place it occupied in the social world. Their efforts in this direction elevated the levels of their own cultural endeavors and, in one way or another, penetrated all other ranks of society. The wealthy and powerful daimyo of the Edo period built splendid mansions and gardens for themselves, and they were emulated by cultivated samurai. The aesthetic spaces devised by each class for their residences and gardens were designed to suit the standing of the owners. This same tradition of matching cultural activities with social class has continued down to the present and has played a part in the modern development of Japanese residential space.

When the feudal government collapsed in the mid-nineteenth century and the parliamentary government of the Meiji era took its place, many of the great gardens constructed by daimyo families were converted into public parks. Although some changes have been made in them, by and large they remain as they were in the past. Among the most outstanding of these former daimyo gardens are Ritsurin Park in Takamatsu, which formerly belonged to the Matsudaira family; Suizenji Park in Kumamoto, which was once an estate of the Hosokawa family; and Korakuen Park in Okayama, which was owned by the Ikeda family, lords of the Bizen fief.

Ritsurin Park (Figs. 118, 139, 159), occupying an

123. Garden pond with water lilies, Meiji Shrine, Tokyo.

area of 750,000 square meters and set off by a background of deep-green mountains, truly expresses a dignity and grandeur suitable for the estate of a feudal lord. Its six ponds offer a wide range of scenic charm, but most lavish from the garden-design point of view is the area around the recently reconstructed Kikugetsu-tei pavilion. In this part of the garden, unusual stones and Judas trees have been used in abundance.

The garden of Suizenji Park (Fig. 96) is distinguished by its masses of carefully trimmed shrubbery and its great expanses of lawn covering a range of artificial hillocks that represent mountains. One of these hillocks was shaped to resemble Mount Fuji, and for that reason, in later years, the garden acquired the popular name of Garden of

the Fifty-three Stations because it was thought to evoke images of the fifty-three post stations on the Tokaido highway, which ran past this most famous of all Japanese mountains. In fact, however, the original intent of the design seems to have been to make the artificial hills a foreground for the scenery in the distance instead of serving as major points of interest in themselves. The *shoin*-style building that fronts on the pond is known as the Hall of Traditional and Modern Learning because it is said to have been the place where Prince Toshihito, builder of the Katsura villa, received instruction from the scholar Hosokawa Yusai. It formerly stood in Kyoto but in later years was removed to its present site.

Rikugien Park in Tokyo (Figs. 95, 119) is part of

a garden constructed in the early eighteenth century by Yanagisawa Yoshiyasu, friend and adviser to the fifth Tokugawa shogun, Tsunayoshi. The controlling idea of the garden was to present in landscape terms the famous scenes mentioned in the *Kokin Wakashu* (Collection of Ancient and Modern Times), the celebrated early-tenth-century anthology of Japanese poetry. The name of the garden itself derives from the same source. In the gently curving edge of the pond, the expanses of smooth lawn, and the handsome forms of numerous pine trees, a generally poetic mood still persists today.

Korakuen Park in Tokyo, like its namesake in Okayama, was once part of a daimyo's garden (Figs. 94, 120). It is a survival of the garden that once surrounded a subordinate mansion of the important Mito branch of the house of Tokugawa.

Today it is sadly spoiled because the city has steadily encroached upon it and polluted its environment. Nevertheless, it remains an unusual garden because its designer Shu Shunsui, Confucian scholar and teacher of the noted Tokugawa Mitsukuni (1638–1700), grandson of the shogun Ieyasu and a leader of distinction in his own right, incorporated Chinese motifs into its design. Among these motifs are the stone bridge patterned after the Chinese half-moon bridge and the stone dike that strives to suggest the famous West Lake scenery of Hangchow (Fig. 94). The central pond, however, is traditionally Japanese in the manner of gardens designed for strolling. There is a waterfall stone group as well as a representation of the Isles of the Blest. On the shore is an artificial hill covered entirely with bamboo grass (Fig. 120). This

△ *124. Guest room, veranda, and garden, Shisen-do, Kyoto.*

125. Stone-paved approach to Jiko-in, Yamato Koriyama, Nara Prefecture.

is probably the most exceptional part of the whole design.

All of the gardens that we have just noted were designed as stroll gardens. It was their purpose to present the viewer with an almost endless succession of attractive vistas as he walked along their paths. Today, even though they are no longer the private gardens of feudal lords, they still perform their original function.

GARDENS OF
THE SAMURAI

As examples of the distinctive spaces created for their residences and gardens by artistically inclined members of the samurai class, the Shisen-do, built by Ishikawa Jozan, and the Jiko-in, built by Katagiri Sekishu, are particularly notable.

Ishikawa Jozan, a member of the seventeenth-century literati—men who were especially devoted to the Chinese classics and to poetry—built the Shisen-do at the foot of the Higashiyama range of hills in Kyoto. Both the residence and the garden are in an excellent state of preservation today, and they give a clear idea of the world that Jozan considered ideal (Figs. 124, 138). The low-level floor of the building connects directly with a gravel-spread area surrounded by closely clipped azaleas (Fig. 138). A single old sasanqua tree casts its shadow on the bright garden and the area under the eaves of the building. In the stream bed at the edge of the garden is a special Japanese device called a *shishi-odoshi*: a hollow segment of bamboo on a hinged framework set beneath a flume that pours water into it. When the water reaches a certain level, the bamboo pipe tips end up, empties the water, and, in returning to its original position, strikes a stone beneath it and produces a pleasant clacking sound. This occasional sound and the fragrance of the sasanqua flowers contribute greatly to the poetic atmosphere of the garden. Especially when one sits at twilight in the room facing the garden, the serenity and calm beauty of the setting suggest how lofty the spiritual qualities of Ishikawa Jozan must have been.

The noted samurai and tea master Katagiri Sekishu built the Jiko-in at Yamato Koriyama in Nara Prefecture as a place of retirement where he could pray that his ancestors might attain Buddhahood. Every aspect of the residence and the garden demonstrates the bold courage and skill of this man (Figs. 98, 125, 157). The approach path, for example, resembles the one designed by Kobori Enshu for the Koho-an, but it is stronger in design and more forceful in expression (Fig. 125). Paved with rough-surfaced stones, it turns at sharp angles and seems to draw the visitor along in its direction of advance. At its end, however, there is the contrast of a gentle thatch-roofed *shoin* building in a rustic style. The open garden, using the borrowed-scenery technique, incorporates an imposing vista of the Yamato Plain into its design. Facing each other on the east and west sides of the garden are a low clipped hedge and large, round mounds of closely clipped shrubbery. The bold, clean design permits an unbroken view of the plain and the distant mountains beyond. At the same time the garden vividly suggests the personality of the designer. For the sake of the view, the east and south sides of the *shoin* building can be thrown completely open. In this manner, the distant landscape is tightly incorporated into the garden design. Even today this carefully devised spatial composition has lost none of its artistic freshness.

BORROWED SCENERY   The Japanese people are innately fond of natural scenery, and for this reason, even though it is uncertain who first used the technique of *shakkei*, or borrowed scenery, or when the technique originated, the idea of "borrowing" distant landscapes

and using them as integral parts of garden designs is very old. In fact, instead of attempting to trace its beginnings, it might be closer to the point simply to consider this approach to garden design as part of the Japanese attitude toward daily life.

Still, although the concept of a garden with a view has been an aspect of Japanese culture for countless ages, the deliberate integration of distant scenery into the design of a garden is a later development that probably dates from no earlier than the Muromachi period. Furthermore, the idea was not perfected as a technique until the late feudal period, or roughly the beginning of the seventeenth century—the time of Kobori Enshu, who did much to crystallize and popularize the technique.

It was around this time that the Chinese writer Li Chi-cheng produced a manual of garden design called *Yuan-yeh* (in Japanese, *En'ya*), in which he divided the technique of borrowing scenery into four categories: borrowing from a distance, borrowing from nearby, borrowing from a high angle, and borrowing from a low angle. Whether his book was directly known in seventeenth-century Japan is uncertain, although it seems likely that its contents, at any rate, might have been part of the general Confucian and Zen culture that was imported before the time when the Tokugawa shogunate closed the country to almost all contacts with the outside world. Nor is it surprising that a distinctly Japanese borrowed-scenery technique developed independent of the dispersal of this kind of Chinese knowledge. We have already noted the borrowed-scenery designs of the Shinju-an at the Daitoku-ji, the Jiko-in, and, most notably, of Shugaku-in. In addition to these, the gardens of the Kyoto temples Entsu-ji and Shoden-ji deserve special mention.

The Entsu-ji occupies the site of the emperor Gomizuno-o's former villa at Hataeda, which the emperor Reigen (reigned 1663–87) later converted into a Buddhist nunnery for his foster mother, Enko-in. The garden, a handsome composition of moss and low stones, is surrounded on three sides by a low hedge. On one side, beyond the hedge and a group of tall trees, lies the borrowed scenery: an imposing view of Mount Hiei (Fig. 126).

126. Detail of garden, with borrowed scenery of Mount Hiei in background, Entsu-ji, Kyoto.

127. *Garden pond and borrowed scenery (Great South Gate of Todai-ji temple), Isui-en, Nara.*

Although today the surrounding cryptomeria trees have grown so tall that the garden is slightly dark in mood, it is quite possible that it was once a bright and open dry-landscape design.

The garden of the Shoden-ji, which also uses Mount Hiei as its borrowed scenery (Figs. 97, 133), differs greatly in design from that of the Entsu-ji. It is surrounded by a clay wall topped with tile and is spread with white gravel in which are placed stones and well-pruned clumps of azalea. This interesting composition produces a fresh and pleasing effect that is unique among Japanese garden designs. The design, like many others, is attributed to Kobori Enshu, but there are no records to substantiate the attribution.

GARDENS OF THE MEIJI ERA

Toward the close of the Edo period—that is, from the early to the mid-nineteenth century—the Japanese garden, like almost all other aspects of Japanese art, became stereotyped and degenerate. The fall of the Tokugawa shogunate and the establishment of a new form of government under the emperor Meiji (whose reign lasted from 1868 to 1912 and is known as the Meiji era) opened Japan to contact with the rest of the world. This sequence of events created a new aristocracy and new persons of power who in turn instigated a variety of movements in many fields of activity. In the garden, too, great changes took place. First of all, copies of Western-style gardens were needed as settings for the new Western-style buildings that were going up in increasing numbers. Second, the new aristocracy and the business magnates launched a wide-scale program of garden planning and construction. Although the activities of these people were startling in their vigor and speed, they lacked the creativity to initiate a new age in art. Still, to surpass mere copying and slavish adherence to established patterns is never easy in any age. In any case, certain gardens of the Meiji era deserve attention because they have an undeniable freshness about them, even though they may be rather subdued in tone.

The garden of the Hoshun-in, located immediately north of the Daisen-in garden at the Daitoku-ji, is particularly noted for its Chinese bellflowers (Fig. 137). Here a plot of ground in front of the abbot's quarters is filled with these plants in a characteristically Japanese composition that is reminiscent of the bush-clover garden at the Kyoto Imperial Palace. The ground cover is moss, and a single line of steppingstones draws the design together and heightens its loveliness. No one can say with certainty when the garden assumed its present appearance or who decided to plant it in this fashion, but it seems that it is not very old. The idea of a garden planted with Chinese bellflowers that bloom only once a year is very much in rapport with modern aesthetic thought.

The iris garden at the Meiji Shrine in Tokyo is another example of a design that depends for its effect on flowers that bloom only once a year (Fig. 142). The site was formerly that of a villa owned by the Kato family, daimyo of the Kumamoto fief. In the seventeenth century it passed into the ownership of the Ii family, and finally, in 1890, it became an imperial property. The estate assumed approximately its present form five years later, when the emperor Meiji ordered extensive reconstruction to transform it into a villa for his consort.

Sparkling water flows from a spring called the Seisho Well through a winding belt of irises to empty into a pond where water lilies grow (Fig. 123). The garden space is surrounded by a deep grove of various kinds of trees. The prevailing mood of the garden is that of natural scenery—scenery, in fact, that is associated with that of the Musashino area in the environs of Tokyo. Great care was needed to cultivate the more than one thousand iris plants of over two hundred varieties —some of them quite old—to their present state of splendor. In June, when the plants burst into thousands of richly colored blossoms, they create a scene of almost unworldly beauty. The pond serves two functions. When the irises are not in bloom, it forms the center of attraction. When they come to flower, it is transformed into an approach to the mystic world of blossoms.

The Murin-an garden in Kyoto (Figs. 121, 122, 143), which was built by the master designer Jihei Ogawa for the great military and political leader Aritomo Yamagata during the 1890's, is an excellent example of a relatively modern garden that represents a blend of traditional technique and creative composition. The garden site, which is near the famous Zen temple Nanzen-ji, is an elongated triangle of no great area. But the skill with which Ogawa used the topography to develop a deep garden was truly outstanding for its time. The view across the pond from in front of the residence seems especially deep because it makes use of borrowed scenery. Beyond the gently rolling lawn, which occupies most of the garden and is cut by two small streams, the Higashiyama range of hills is visible in the distance (Fig. 122). The streams and the pond are fed by a spring that was already on the site and by water piped in from a canal that flows from Lake Biwa. Because of the abundance of water, it was possible to create not only the streams and the pond but also a waterfall. Somehow the quiet gurgling of the water in the deep tranquility of the garden seems to calm the spirit and at the same time to bring to mind concepts of garden design that had been undergoing refinement since the Heian age. Here the famous garden designer Jihei Ogawa, working according to the tastes of Aritomo Yamagata himself, produced a symbol of one aspect of the Meiji-era culture.

CHAPTER SIX

Space and Form
in Japanese Gardens

THE INTEGRATION OF INTERIOR AND EXTERIOR SPACE Because of its predominantly warm, moist climate, Japan developed a form of wooden architecture characterized by an extreme openness of structure and, in this respect, quite different from the traditional stone and brick architecture of the West. It goes almost without saying that this architecture was distinctively Japanese. But the desire for good ventilation and cooling breezes in hot weather was not the only motive that prompted the development of open-structure buildings. The characteristic Japanese love of nature and the desire for intimate contact with it in daily life also provided strong motivation. In fact, closeness to nature has formed the basis of all Japanese culture. It has been the definitive element in Japanese spatial composition in both architecture and garden design, and it has enabled the Japanese to create their own distinctive aesthetic world.

The *shoin* building of the Jiko-in (Figs. 98, 128, 129) displays openness of structure in an extremely bold manner. For the sake of the view, as we have already noted, both the east and the south sides of the main room are completely open (except, of course, when weather conditions require the replacement of the *shoji*) in what amounts to a classic expression of the ideal Japanese daily-life space.

There is nothing between roof and floor but a few slender structural posts, and no partitions delineate the boundary between interior and exterior. In fact, interior and exterior in the Western sense do not exist, for the two are united. The only factors that make such a distinction in the room at the Jiko-in are light and shade and textural modulation. The textures of materials underfoot vary from that of the reed-and-grass mats of the room to that of the wooden-floored veranda and then to that of the white gravel with which the garden is spread. The progression stops at the clipped hedge on the far side of the garden, but up to that point it is an unbroken spatial continuity. The nature of the materials overhead is similarly modulated: first, the ceiling and then the undersides of the eaves, but from there on, the boundless sky. In other words, there is no clear spatial delineation, even though different areas exist in a psychological but not a physical sense. The organic unity of architecture and garden, which together create the psychological realms, derives from an important aspect of the Japanese national personality. In short, whereas the Westerner thinks in terms of opposed architectural and outdoor spaces, the Japanese thinks of his home as a unity of room and garden.

A residential building in the ancient *shinden* style

128. Jiko-in, Yamato Koriyama, Nara Prefecture.

consisted of two major parts: a *moya*, or central space, and surrounding spaces called *hisashi*. Structural posts stood on the line of junction between these two, but no permanent partitions divided the one from the other. When they were needed, blinds called *sudare* could be hung in the interpost spaces. Nevertheless, in spite of the lack of doors and walls or partitions, different functions and daily-life order strictly and clearly separated the *moya* from the *hisashi*.

In the later *shoin* architectural style, the introduction of sliding panels—*fusuma* (sliding interior partitions), *shoji,* and wooden doors—to divide room from room heightened the independence of spaces. But these partitions, flimsy at best, did no more than provide visual obstruction. The transoms above them were either entirely or largely open, and therefore true privacy did not exist. Still, the class distinctions of the feudal society that employed this architectural tradition preserved very clear abstract distinctions among rooms.

Such distinctions have for many centuries constituted the major element in Japanese spatial consciousness. Without employing definite physical means of separation or enclosure, the Japanese have come to understand different spaces as psychologically independent. An extreme example of this attitude is to be found at the Shinto shrine, where a sacred precinct is marked off by no more than a straw rope decorated with a few folded strips of white paper. This rope cannot keep out intruders, but from the psychological standpoint the Japanese recognize it as establishing an inviolable holy zone.

The Japanese approach amounts to delineating a precinct by means of drawing a single line. There are many instances of such a line represented by many different things devised to suit the requirements of the immediate condition. At the Shinto shrine, a rope is symbolically sufficient to the purpose. For other needs, however, the line may take the form of a hedge or a thick stone or clay wall. To further illustrate my meaning, let me turn once more to the Jiko-in.

The floor- and ground-level progression from the *shoin* building through the garden moves across *tatami* mats, board flooring, and a spread of white gravel to be terminated at the clipped hedge. On further consideration, however, one sees that the space of the Jiko-in is by no means cut off at the hedge, for one's eye is free to travel all the way to the Yamato Mountains in the remote distance. To be sure, this vast space can be interpreted as no more than a view, but in this case "view" is inadequate to express all the influences that the whole region exerts on the Jiko-in. The effect of the distant scene is not merely visual but also includes light, wind, rain, snow, heat, cold, sound, and smell—all of which participate in the daily life of those who live there. In short, the view is infinitely more than a painted mural intended merely to be observed.

The spaces of the Jiko-in are divided by three boundaries into three different stages. The distant range of mountains establishes the first stage, the clipped hedge at the far side of the garden the second, and the under-eaves area—that is, the veranda—the third. Although these boundaries are themselves extremely vague, the spaces they establish are definite entities. Perhaps "boundaries" is inadequate here, but it is difficult to find a word that conveys the function of these dividing lines. They are not true boundaries because they at once separate one zone from another and unite the two. Nevertheless, an understanding of their role is essential to a comprehension of the development of Japanese aesthetics, for skillful manipulation of forms combining the roles of division and integration is the most important characteristic of Japanese spatial composition.

In Japanese architecture, the elements that simultaneously divide and unite interior space and

130. Tsukimi-dai *(moon-viewing platform)*, Old Shoin, Katsura villa, Kyoto.

garden are the veranda and the eaves, which are treated in a distinctive way. These architectural devices, developed through a long tradition of refinement and change and basically unlike their Western counterparts, impart subtle nuances to the spaces they define. They have enriched and varied the spatial composition of Japanese residences of the late feudal and the modern age, as is probably best exemplified in the buildings of the Katsura villa. In this respect, possibly the most truly Japanese feature of the Katsura buildings is the so-called *tsukimi-dai*, or moon-viewing platform, which projects into the garden from the front of the Old Shoin (Fig. 130).

The veranda to which the moon-viewing platform is attached is floored with boards, but the upper surface of the platform itself is composed of closely placed bamboo poles laid in parallel formation. Why should this simple exposed rec-

tangular platform appeal strongly to the Japanese mind? I am convinced that the sole reason is to be found in its nature as a bright, light-drenched link between interior space and the exterior world of nature. This roofless platform is at once an extension of the interior floor and a part of the garden. It is one with both the dimly lighted room inside and the brilliant space of the outdoors. Although in terms of position it is in the garden, because it is an extension of the flooring it is intimately connected with the interior area. The high elevation of the floor of the Old Shoin (Fig. 71) inevitably produces a clear distinction between interior and exterior space, but the moon-viewing platform organically connects them.

The selection of bamboo poles as the flooring material makes the moon-viewing platform eminently successful in achieving this effect. If the designer had chosen to build a stone terrace, for

131. Middle Shoin and adjacent garden area, Katsura villa, Kyoto.

example, the effect would have been so heavy that the platform would have seemed completely divorced from the building, which of course is light in general mood. On the other hand, bamboo laid in straight rows creates the needed link. The ability to achieve effects like this is part of the wisdom in design and craftsmanship that has developed out of the traditional Japanese way of life.

An interesting example of a similar process in reverse can be seen in the Shoi-ken teahouse at Katsura. Whereas the moon-viewing platform of the Old Shoin is an example of extending the interior space and modulating its textures to blend with those of the garden, the earth-floored area under the eaves of the Shoi-ken (Fig. 132) shows how the designer has allowed the natural exterior ground surface to penetrate into what is in fact architectural space. Eaves supported by free-standing posts project from the main body of the building and well beyond the board-floored veranda. In other words, the natural earth and stones of the

exterior are introduced into a covered architectural zone as a link between inside and outside. Although the Shokin-tei and the Gepparo teahouses at Katsura also employ this modulating device, their versions of it are less strikingly effective than that of the Shoi-ken.

The refined and subtle tradition of tea that inspired the development of *sukiya* architecture, which reached its pinnacle in the Katsura villa, often borrowed rustic elements from farmhouses and, after subjecting them to a process of refinement, employed them in teahouse and residential design. The deep eaves and the earth-floored area beneath them, as exemplified in the Shoi-ken, are a case in point. This idea evolved from the *doma,* an earth-floored interior space lying beyond the entrance to the traditional Japanese farmhouse or urban commoner's house. In keeping with the rustic nature of its origin, structures in the *sukiya* style are usually supported on round log posts instead of the finished posts common in residences

132. *Under-eaves area and stone-paved walk, Shoi-ken teahouse, Katsura villa, Kyoto.*

133. *Dry-landscape garden, stone-filled gutter, and veranda, abbot's quarters, Shoden-ji, Kyoto.*

134 (opposite page, left). Approach path and hedge of ▷
interwoven bamboo, Katsura villa, Kyoto.

135 (opposite page, right). Approach path and bamboo ▷
fence, Katsura villa, Kyoto.

in the *shoin* style. In many instances the bark is left on the logs, but sometimes it is removed and the logs are polished. This approach to the use of structural materials is similar to the one that employed unfinished bamboo for the moon-viewing platform of the Old Shoin. In both cases, material in its natural state is deliberately employed to mediate between interior and garden.

Forming the ground-level boundary and junction between the tea garden and the under-eaves area of the Shoi-ken is a straight line of pavement composed of large roundish stones at the sides and smaller stones at the center (Fig. 132). This pavement ends at a point directly below the end of the eaves. The steppingstones placed almost carelessly in the earth-floored area under the eaves and the attractively shaped ritual water basin next to one of the corner posts merely serve to beautify the connecting zone. Spatially the most important element is the interval between the pavement and the entrance to the interior of the teahouse. The breadth of the earth-floored area and the depth

of shadow created by the broadly projecting eaves give life to the design. This shadowed space plays an important role in the gradual psychological adjustment necessary to prepare the mind and heart for participation in the tea ceremony.

The interior of the traditional teahouse, unlike most Japanese interiors, is almost entirely shut off from the outside world. This is as it must be for the purpose of the tea ceremony, which requires intense spiritual concentration. But creating an abrupt shift from the open space of the garden to the tightly enclosed zone of the tearoom would not generate the spiritual attitude required. A more gradual modulation must be devised. The tea garden is itself part of the world of the tea ceremony in that it must lead the participant from the distractions of mundane life into the serenity of the tearoom. For this reason it too must be enclosed in such a way as to block off all views that would disturb the mind. Between exterior spaces and the closed-off interior space there must be a point of transition. At the Shoi-ken and at other similar

buildings, the spatial and spiritual gradation is provided by the shadowy earth-floored area under the eaves. With no break in mood, this zone combines interior and exterior both in materials and in lighting. The participant in the tea ceremony is thus led from the clamor of the outside world to the tranquility of the tea garden. Then he passes through the shadowed under-eaves area, where he further prepares his mind for the even more shadowy tearoom with its low sliding-door entrance, through which he passes by crouching down, and perhaps one or two *shoji*-covered windows.

The problem of linking interior and exterior is solved in Japanese architecture by the skillful manipulation of the two extremes of light and dark. The moon-viewing platform of the Old Shoin projects from the building into the garden as if in search of light. On the other hand, the earth-floored area under the eaves of the Shoi-ken creates shadow in order to invite the tea-ceremony participant into a still dimmer interior. These two architectural devices reveal the extremes of the com-

plex traditional technique for composing space.

But the earth-floored under-eaves area is used in many other buildings outside the mainstream of the enclosed teahouse. For instance, the Rin'un-tei pavilion in the spacious and open Upper Garden of the Shugaku-in villa has a similar earth-floored area (Fig. 2). In this case, however, the required element is not the shadow that is essential at the Shoi-ken but a softened light that enables the viewer of the sweeping scene to feel as if the world of nature were blending with his own attitudes toward life.

The spatial difference between the under-eaves zones at the Shoi-ken and the Rin'un-tei results from the way the ground has been treated. In contrast with the straight line of pavement and the numerous large steppingstones placed in darkish natural earth at the Shoi-ken, the ground under the eaves of the Rin'un-tei is covered with an almost white mortarlike substance called *tataki* that is ornamented with groups of two or three colored pebbles in a widely spaced overall pattern. Clearly

136. Hedge-enclosed approach to Upper Garden, Shugaku-in villa, Kyoto.

the aim of the former is the creation of shadow, while that of the latter is the generation of brightness. These two examples show the opposing uses to which the same modulating device can be put to create radically different moods. There are many similar examples in Japanese architecture.

At the Jiko-in the large south and east openings in the building play the most important role in unifying interior space and the garden (Fig. 129). The impression produced by the composition would be entirely different if only one of these sides was open. But Japanese architecture, in accordance with the situation, makes good use of the effects of both one-side and two-side openings in construction and garden design. The Seiryo-den of the Kyoto Imperial Palace comes into direct contact with the bush-clover garden only on the west side. A similar instance is the Taizo-in garden

attributed to Kano Motonobu, but here a low wall at the edge of the veranda further weakens the connection. The reason for this design approach is to be found in the nature of the spaces. In both instances the garden is intended to be viewed from a seated position inside the building, and it exerts no influence on daily life. Both spaces are fundamentally static. The spatial mood of the Jiko-in contrasts strongly with these two because the two wide openings suggest that the garden is dynamically related to the daily life of the people who inhabit the building.

Still, it is possible to have gardens onto which buildings open on two sides without generating this dynamic feeling. The abbot's quarters at the Daitoku-ji and the Shinju-an both open on their gardens on the south and the east; at the Ryoan-ji, on the south and the west; and at the Daisen-in,

137. Detail of Chinese-bellflower garden, Hoshun-in, Daitoku-ji, Kyoto.

138. *View of garden from guest room, Shisen-do, Kyoto.*

139. Southern pond and Kikugetsu-tei pavilion, Ritsurin Park, Takamatsu, Kagawa Prefecture.

140. *Steppingstones in front of waiting bench in tea garden, Fushin-an, Omote Senke school of tea, Kyoto.*

142. *View of iris garden, Meiji Shrine, Tokyo.*

143. *Garden pond, Murin-an, Kyoto.*

144. *Detail of moat and embankment, Tokyo Imperial Palace.*

145. *Hedge-enclosed approach to Jisho-ji, Kyoto.*

on the east and the north. But in none of these instances is actual connection effected on two sides, since the garden exists independently as a separate entity when seen from either side. Indeed, in each case the garden is deliberately designed to be seen from one opening at a time.

Simultaneous double-opening connections with garden spaces are more common in buildings of the *shoin* tradition. Buildings in the older *shinden* style were marked by a certain spatial frontality that rendered them to some extent static and dictated a one-side connection with the garden area (Fig. 22). In the *shoin* style, however, and in the later *sukiya* style, a staggered placement of the component buildings—as seen in the arrangement at the Katsura villa and the Ninomaru compound of Nijo Castle—stimulated a new kind of spatial awareness in which the interior and the daily life of the occupants came to have a more intimate relation, both visually and dynamically, with the garden. As a matter of fact, this awareness is one of the clearest expressions of the ideas behind the *shoin* style.

GARDENS AND ENCLOSURES

As we have noted above, the traditional Japanese house does not guarantee privacy within its own boundaries. Interestingly enough, however, the Japanese garden originates in the idea of insuring privacy, since it inevitably comes into being only after a certain area has been enclosed by a fence or a wall. The enclosed space must consist of both the building and the garden existing as a unity. In speaking of enclosed space, of course, I do not mean a tightly sealed area but an area that is coherent in mood. Consequently, the form of the enclosing element may vary from the massive stone ramparts of castles to hedges and lightweight fences of widely spaced bamboo poles. Selecting the form of the enclosing element is the initial step from which all further planning of spatial compositions proceeds.

From ancient to modern times, the tile-topped clay wall has been the most common enclosure for residential buildings and temples because it is durable and strong enough to deter intruders. For this reason it gradually came to symbolize power

and social status, and from the times when court nobles erected huge *shinden*-style mansions it served as the standard type of enclosure for gardens.

As long as the garden is extensive, the wall need do no more than perform the function of a barrier between the garden area and the world beyond, but when it surrounds only a small space, it becomes the background of the garden itself. In small spaces like the bush-clover garden at the Kyoto Imperial Palace, the clay wall defines the nature of the space, and the skill, or lack of skill, with which it is treated determines the success or failure of the design.

There are many Japanese gardens in which clay walls serve effectively as backgrounds, but none are more outstanding in this respect than the stone gardens of the Ryoan-ji (Figs. 78, 79) and the Daisen-in (Figs. 73, 75). At the Daisen-in, where the garden is very shallow, the mass and the whiteness of the wall bring the large boat-shaped stone to startling life. At the Ryoan-ji the low, thick surrounding wall binds together a number of stone groups that might otherwise tend to look widely scattered. Moreover, the mystical quality and the quiet color tones that the latter wall has acquired with age serve to emphasize the beauty of the stone-group placement. The clay wall of the Shoden-ji garden (Fig. 97) performs a slightly different function. Although it constitutes a background to set off the closely clipped forms of the azaleas, it also marks the boundary between the white-gravel garden space and the distant view of Mount Hiei that is borrowed and incorporated into the garden design. A view of this same mountain forms the borrowed scenery of the Entsu-ji garden (Fig. 126), but a comparison of the use of the borrowed-scenery technique in the two garden compositions reveals several interesting differences. First of all, the garden components are different. Whereas a white clay wall is the boundary line between garden and borrowed scenery at the Shoden-ji, a pruned hedge serves this purpose at the Entsu-ji. And in place of the white gravel and clipped azaleas in the former, stone groups and moss are used in the latter. The differences in garden components inevitably reflect basically different ideas about gar-

146 (opposite page, left). Stone-paved walk and interior hedge, Taizo-in, Myoshin-ji, Kyoto.

147 (opposite page, right). Stone-paved approach to Old Shoin, Katsura villa, Kyoto.

148. Steppingstone arrangement at main entrance to Old Shoin, Katsura villa, Kyoto.

den spaces and particularly about borrowing outside scenic elements. At the Shoden-ji, the concept of borrowed scenery is less well developed than it is at the Entsu-ji.

The starting point of the Shoden-ji plan is the concept of using a clay wall to enclose the garden space in front of the abbot's quarters. The design then modulates the garden forms to agree with the form of Mount Hiei, which remains symbolically as well as actually in the distance. The ground cover of white gravel is a standard element in gardens located in front of buildings like the abbot's quarters, and the shapes of the closely clipped azaleas are a subtle harmonizing factor among gravel, wall, and remote mountain. As a device for achieving its specific end, the Shoden-ji composition succeeds for the reason that if the azaleas were to be replaced by stones—in short, if it were possible to duplicate at the Shoden-ji a composition like that of the Ryoan-ji garden—a patent discord would arise between garden and mountain.

In contrast with the basic approach of the Shoden-ji garden, that of the Entsu-ji garden originates in the desire to lay primary stress on the view of Mount Hiei. Consequently, the clay wall has been rejected as unacceptable. Such a wall, because of its extremely space-defining nature, would keep the mountain in the distance and limit the expansiveness of the garden space. Lacking a rigid sense of spatial definition, the hedge, because of its generally soft quality, satisfactorily includes the distant mountain in the garden space. The stones in front of the hedge add a stern note of strength, but the ground cover of moss softens this to harmonize it with the view of the mountain. The conceptual process in which this garden design evolved consisted essentially of three phases: the use of a hedge to permit incorporation of a distant scene, the addition of stones for strength and for reinforcement of the softness of the hedge, and the use of a ground cover of velvety moss to alleviate the severity of the stones.

Other outstanding examples of the hedge used as an intermediary element to draw borrowed scenery into the garden are to be seen at the Shugaku-in villa (Fig. 36) and the Jiko-in (Fig. 129),

but in neither case does the nature of the topography require a clay wall to delineate space and insure privacy. At Shugaku-in the hedge covers the outer face of a huge dike, and at the Jiko-in it stands at the edge of a bluff below which lies a reservoir. For that matter, no clay wall is needed at the Entsu-ji either, since the land outside the garden is at a lower level than the garden itself.

When topographical conditions are less propitious, as in the Murin-an garden (Figs. 121, 122), a clay wall is used, but it is concealed by means of trees and shrubbery. Here, since a low hedge would be insufficient for the purpose of incorporating the borrowed scenery, plants of considerable size are needed. Again, in order to prevent the trees from overpowering the borrowed scenery, they must stand at some distance from the main vantage point. In this respect, the depth of the Murin-an garden has been put to excellent use.

Sometimes, when the mass and weight of a clay wall would be out of keeping with the composition, hedges are used in designs that do not employ the borrowed-scenery technique. Two of the most noteworthy of such designs are those of the Katsura villa and the Temple of the Silver Pavilion. The famous bamboo hedge at Katsura (Fig. 134) has been created by weaving young living bamboo plants into a framework so that, from the front, it seems to be a solid mass of foliage. It thus blends perfectly with the atmosphere of a villa built as a place of refuge from the bustle and dirt of a large city. Since the back of the hedge is unsightly—a vast collection of bamboo stems bent to form a framework—such a device could only be used in gardens of great size where the view from the rear need not be taken into consideration. The hedge at the Temple of the Silver Pavilion (Fig. 145) could perhaps more accurately be called a fence.

149 (opposite page, left). Stone-paved walk, with Shokin-tei teahouse in background, Katsura villa, Kyoto.

150 (opposite page, right). Sun disc (foreground) and lotus-shaped pond (background), Hompo-ji, Kyoto.

151. Stone mortars used as steppingstones in pond, Isui-en, Nara.

It is a three-part composition in which the lowest course is a wall of rough stone masonry, the second a fence of split bamboo, and the third a tall hedge formed of trees. Running along a gravel-spread walk that takes one ninety-degree turn and then continues in a long straight line, this hedge-fence evokes a feeling of dignity and sophistication without suggesting the cold severity of a tile-topped clay wall. Its mood seems to recall the high level and excellent taste of the Higashiyama culture, of which the temple itself is a brilliant product.

Some fences and hedges, unlike enclosures that insure privacy by surrounding an entire site, serve only to establish spatial divisions within the site. They may set off one part of it as a garden, or they may separate one kind of garden space from another. Such fences and hedges and the wide variety of gates and other entranceways employed with them are most frequently found in tea gardens, where they divide the outer approach from the inner one that leads to the teahouse itself. Since they serve primarily a psychological function, they are often soft in appearance. Concealing hedges and light bamboo constructions are especially popular. Some of the most effective uses of this kind of partitioning element are to be seen in the vicinity of the Miyukimon (Gate of the Imperial Visit) at the Katsura villa, where very light and delicate bamboo fences and gates delineate certain areas while hedges lead the eye in lines along which the designer intended one to look. Although the total atmosphere created by these fences and hedges is warm and gentle, they nonetheless strictly establish spatial divisions.

Hedges primarily conceal. They either cut off views from the outside or hide things that are not considered necessary in the garden. There is one kind of hedge, however, that is completely orna-

152. Stone bridge in front of Shokin-tei teahouse, Katsura villa, Kyoto.

153 (opposite page, left). Steppingstone approach to ▷ Fushin-an teahouse, Omote Senke school of tea, Kyoto.

154 opposite (page, right). Boat landing, northern ▷ pond, Sento Imperial Palace garden, Kyoto.

mental in function. Because it is low, it is sometimes called a skirt hedge or a handrail hedge. A number of Japanese gardens, including the one at the Taizo-in (Fig. 146), make excellent use of this purely decorative hedge.

SPATIAL BALANCE Since the Japanese garden has developed principally around the idea of natural scenery, it takes one of three forms: a miniaturized version of a natural scene, a copy of part of a natural scene, or a symbolic, abstract representation of a natural scene. Consequently, the geometrical patterns found in most Western gardens display an aesthetic fundamentally alien to the Japanese personality. The Japanese ideal of beauty is most often expressed in asymmetry. Such expression can be seen in the development of Japanese architecture as well. Temple and residential styles imported from China in

the fifth and sixth centuries invariably revealed the Chinese fondness for symmetrical arrangement. For example, the standard continental Buddhist temple was constructed symmetrically on a straight north-south axis. The *shinden*-style mansions of ancient Japan were based on a Chinese model in which the main section of the structure faced south and was flanked by subordinate structures in symmetrical placement. The initial step in adapting these forms to the Japanese milieu involved the breaking of the bonds of symmetry and the positioning of architectural components according to Japanese preference and the requirements of topography. Naturally, garden design followed a similar trend. Over the centuries, the concept of asymmetry in art became so deeply ingrained in Japanese aesthetic thinking that in the medieval age, when Zen Buddhism gained wide popularity and a heavily Chinese-influenced Zen architectural

style came to be used for temples of the sect, symmetrical placement was employed only in the vicinity of the major Buddha hall. Even in places like the small gardens facing the abbots' quarters, the forms and spaces were balanced in an asymmetrical fashion. The only instances of Chinese right-left symmetry employed in Japan in later periods were deliberate copies symbolizing some special attitude.

One such copy is the Confucian temple of the Shizutani School in Okayama Prefecture (Fig. 155). This school was established in the Edo period by the Bizen fief to serve as a center of Confucian learning for its retainers. The temple building and its compound are extremely Chinese in design. A white clay wall topped with red tile surrounds the compound, and a gentle and perfectly straight flight of steps leads to the centrally placed front gate. On either side of the steps is a tree said to

have been raised from seed brought from trees growing at the tomb of Confucius in China. Symmetrically placed trees were traditional in certain ancient Japanese palace compounds—for example, the cherry and the mandarin orange in front of the Shishin-den of the Kyoto Imperial Palace (Fig. 22). But it is important to note that this palace usage is also a result of Chinese influence and that Japanese preferences quite early manifested themselves in the rejection of rigid symmetry of this kind. Only when deliberate attempts were made to reproduce a Chinese mood, as in the case of the Shizutani School, did the Japanese make use of strictly symmetrical placement.

As Japanese residential architecture broke with the older *shinden* tradition to develop the native *shoin* style, emphasis came to be placed on balance in asymmetry. But apart from the lessons learned from architectural design, the Japanese had still

155. *Confucian temple, Shizu-tani School, Iri-mura, Okayama Prefecture.*

156 *(opposite page, left). Stone* ▷ *lantern at boat landing in front of Shoi-ken teahouse, Katsura villa, Kyoto.*

157 *(opposite page, right). View* ▷ *of garden with stone water basin in foreground, Jiko-in, Yamato Koriyama, Nara Prefecture.*

earlier training in asymmetrical design, namely in the technique of arranging stones in copies of natural scenes. Even when the idea to be represented was conventional and formalized, like the legendary Isles of the Blest or the Buddhist Mount Sumeru, the materials used were always natural stones and were consequently free, asymmetrical forms. Since no two are ever of exactly the same size or form, stones demand distinctive formal balance in their arrangement. Techniques for dealing with specific sets of stones ultimately developed into standardized styles that gradually became a basic part of all garden design. The classic stone groupings—the Isles of the Blest, Mount Sumeru, the so-called Buddhist triad, or *sanzon*, and the waterfall—added a high degree of refinement to formal beauty evolving from asymmetrical balance. This development in turn gave rise to the free forms represented by steppingstones and stone-paved areas and thus helped to perfect the aesthetic composition of the Japanese garden.

The basic principle of balanced stone groupings calls for a central stone (*shuseki*), a first subordinate stone (*fukuseki*), and a second subordinate stone (*kyakuseki*). The three are most often arranged in the form of a scalene triangle. The *sanzon*, or Buddhist-triad group, frequently the major point of interest in garden compositions, is a basic example of this type of placement. The name probably indicates the aesthetic importance of the arrangement, since it is difficult to believe that all such groups strive to represent three Buddhist images. Many other stone arrangements are based on the same principle and often take the form of a scalene triangle.

The idea of a major element and two subordinate ones extends beyond stone groups to govern entire garden compositions—that is, compositions in which there is generally a major view together with two less important views planned to maintain a triangular relationship. The same principle applies in the art of flower arrangement, where the three elements are referred to as heaven, man, and earth. But just as flower arrangements based

on this idea do not always demand the physical presence of exactly three elements, so considerable variation is permitted in garden compositions. Sometimes there may be two *fukuseki* in a stone group, and sometimes there may be several *kyakuseki*. In such instances two or three stones together form one of the apexes of the scalene triangle. There are even instances in which one of the three elements in the grouping is omitted and a blank space allowed to complete the balance. Again, a *kyakuseki* of one triangular group may be called upon to duplicate its role in conjunction with a *shuseki* and a *fukuseki* of another group. The stone groups at the Ryoan-ji (Fig. 78) and the Shinju-an (Fig. 81) are excellent examples of the use of this technique.

The arrangement of steppingstones and stones for the removal of outdoor footgear—that is, stones placed at the edge of the veranda or the entrance to the teahouse—follows the same triangular principle. In the case of the footgear stones (to coin an English name for them) the largest stands nearest

to the veranda or the tearoom entrance. Next to it, and lower in height, stands another stone, and then, next to this one, another stone still lower in height (Fig. 66). The only difference in principle between this kind of grouping and the Buddhist-triad arrangement is that it serves a practical rather than an ornamental function. Although the footgear stones assume different technical names when they are used at the entrance to a teahouse, the principle of triangular arrangement remains the same (Fig. 117). The placement of steppingstones in the garden is also generally based on the principle of groups of three, but there are a number of variations: connected series of two, three, or four stones; staggered lines; broken groups of two and then three stones; and groupings of seven, five, and three stones.

At the Heian Shrine garden in Kyoto there is an interesting arrangement of steppingstones leading across a pond. The stones are actually cylinders of granite, skillfully placed in a random fashion so that their forms harmonize pleasantly with the water lilies in the pond. A variation of this technique with a distinctive mood of its own is to be seen in the garden of the Isui-en in Nara, where antique stone mortars have been used to form a path across the pond (Fig. 151).

In the modern period, cut and dressed stones, in contrast with stones of natural shape, began to appear in garden designs (Kobori Enshu himself was skillful at using them in new forms), but they tended to introduce a symmetry born of their own shapes. Because the Japanese fundamentally prefer asymmetry, they feel unsatisfied unless the geometrical balance is broken in some fashion. It will be interesting here to glance briefly at the one outstanding—and, to Japanese eyes, odd—example of a geometrically planned garden that uses dressed stones.

The garden of the Hompo-ji in Kyoto contains a circular pond with a border of rectangular dressed stones (Fig. 150). Nearby, flush with the ground, is a stone disc composed of two half-moon segments. Legend has it that this arrangement represents the name of the great thirteenth-century Buddhist leader Nichiren, the stone disc standing for the character *nichi* (sun) and the pond, through its shape, symbolizing a lotus flower and therefore the character *ren* (lotus). In a word, the effect is that of a rebus. Be that as it may, however, the geometric symmetry obviously did not arise from aesthetic awareness alone, and it generally awakens in the Japanese mind a sense of something peculiar because it is unnatural.

Since their presence automatically means the introduction of geometrical straight lines, planes, and regular curves, dressed stones represent an important revolution in gardens that had formerly relied without variation on the free forms of stones in natural shape. Furthermore, the discord that is inevitable in the combined use of natural and processed stones presents difficult problems. Nevertheless, the problems were solved by talented designers, and this mixture of contrasting materials

may be one of the factors that inspired modern Japanese gardens with a new sense of vigor. It is true, however, that in the early stages the successful combination of the two might have been impossible without the genius of a man like Kobori Enshu.

In the boat landings of the Sento Palace garden (Fig. 154) and the Katsura garden (Fig. 156), cut and dressed stones function in two ways: to serve a practical purpose, which is obviously best served by this kind of material, and to provide a visual contrast with the curved lines of the opposite shore. Another example of the masterly use of rectangular stones to enhance a visual effect can be seen in the long footbridge leading across the pond in front of the Shokin-tei teahouse at the Katsura villa (Figs. 92, 103, 152). At one end of the bridge is a stone group set in the water and arranged as a modified ritual water basin. The dynamic composition formed by the straight bridge and the natural stones of this group is one of the most striking sights in the Katsura garden, but the effect would have been greatly weakened if the bridge had been either an earth-topped wooden structure or a natural stone slab of the kind found elsewhere in the garden.

The stone-paved walk leading to the main entrance of the Old Shoin at Katsura takes full advantage of the aesthetic possibilities inherent in straight-line patterns (Figs. 89, 148). Like the above-noted boat landings, this famous pavement, while serving an important functional purpose, surpasses mere practicality to play a vital role in the spatial composition of this part of the garden. Since the functional nature of pavements of this kind runs the danger of being too strongly expressed, combinations of dressed stones with natural stones as a softening element are preferred for the tea garden. As a matter of fact, the paved area of dressed stones at the entrance to the Old Shoin of the Katsura villa is designed to harmonize with the stone steps and the footgear stone at the entryway. It is the only example of such a pave-

---

158. Stone lanterns, Katsura villa, Kyoto. Top to bottom, left to right: ikekomi *style,* ikekomi *style,* Oribe *style,* yukimi *(snow-* ▷
viewing) style, okidoro *(lantern without a pedestal),* yukimi *style,* okidoro, *ikekomi style.*

159. View of garden and Kikugetsu-tei pavilion, with stone water basin in foreground, Ritsurin Park, Takamatsu, Kagawa Prefecture.

ment at Katsura, and even here natural stepping-stones are set in the moss around it to relieve the severity of the tone.

Stone lanterns were originally votive lights placed in front of Buddhist halls like the Phoenix Hall at the Byodo-in (Fig. 28) and the main hall of the Joruri-ji (Fig. 29), but in gardens of the modern period they came to play an ornamental role, serving to highlight certain areas of the general design. In tea gardens they are often used to light the path to the teahouse when tea ceremonies are held at night. In the early period of their use in gardens they were simply borrowed from temples in unchanged form, but later a number of new sculptural forms emerged—all designed specifically for garden use.

Undoubtedly the best place to observe a wide variety of these forms is the garden of the Katsura villa, which has no fewer than twenty-four stone lanterns, each of which has special characteristics of its own. Some are tall, some short, some square,

some round, some hexagonal, and all were selected according to the requirements of their locations in the garden design (Fig. 158). They include the following types: the basic temple type, which is hexagonal in cross section; variations of this type known as the *ikekomi* and the Oribe style (the latter named for the famous tea master Furuta Oribe); the *yukimi* (snow-viewing) type, with widespread legs and a broad top; and the *okidoro* type, which has neither a pedestal nor legs but rests directly on the ground and has never assumed a standard fixed form, thus remaining unique among stone-lantern types.

The ritual water basin, or *chozubachi*, is another example of the use of processed stone in the Japanese garden. Its function, which since ancient times has been considered extremely important, is to invite the visitor to wash his hands and rinse his mouth in a brief act of purification—in a word, to become aware of his own psychological tensions and, through this act, to rid himself of them. The significance of the ritual water basin became all the stronger with the development of the tea garden, where it assumes the name of *tsukubai,* a word indicating that its low height and its placement require the tea-ceremony guest to bend down over it, thereby humbling himself in preparation for the tea ritual. Over the centuries the *tsukubai* has been refined to the point where, even though it is capable of virtually unlimited variation, it always displays great beauty of form.

According to the requirements of the garden design, the ritual water basin may be anything from a natural stone with a depression carved in the top (Fig. 159) to a geometric or sculptured form (Fig. 157). In keeping with the Japanese fondness for harmony with the world of nature, however, even carefully cut geometrical basins are often chipped or broken to reveal a small part of the pristine stone texture. For instance, the basin in front of the *shoin* building at the Jiko-in (Fig. 157) is cut in the shape of a square post, but one corner of the upper surface has been broken away to show the stone in its original rough condition. Here, in the deliberate breaking of a perfect geometrical shape to make it harmonize with the world of nature represented by the garden, we observe an extremely Japanese expression of aesthetic consciousness.

TITLES IN THE SERIES

Although the individual books in the series are designed as self-contained units, so that readers may choose subjects according to their personal interests, the series itself constitutes a full survey of Japanese art and will be of increasing reference value as it progresses. The following titles are listed in the same order, roughly chronological, as those of the original Japanese editions. Those marked with an asterisk (*) have already been published or will appear shortly. It is planned to publish the remaining titles at about the rate of eight a year, so that the English-language series will be complete in 1974.

The "weathermark" identifies this book as having been planned, designed, and produced at the Tokyo offices of John Weatherhill, Inc., 7-6-13 Roppongi, Minato-ku, Tokyo 106. Book design and typography by Meredith Weatherby and Ronald V. Bell. Layout of photographs by Ronald V. Bell and Sigrid Nikovskis. Composition by General Printing Co., Yokohama. Color plates engraved and printed by Nissha Printing Co., Kyoto, and Hanshichi Printing Co., Tokyo. Gravure plates engraved and printed by Inshokan Printing Co., Tokyo. Monochrome letterpress platemaking and printing and text printing by Toyo Printing Co., Tokyo. Bound at the Makoto Binderies, Tokyo. Text is set in 10-pt. Monotype Baskerville with hand-set Optima for display.

5/00   33 5/00

4/02   38   12/01

3/05   (46) 12/04

9/10   (55)   4/10

12/10 (88) 12/15